# OCEANS

## *and* BEACHES

Trevor Day

**www.raintreepublishers.co.uk**
Visit our website to find out more information about Raintree books.

**To order:**
☎ Phone 0845 6044371
▤ Fax +44 (0) 1865 312263
✉ Email myorders@raintreepublishers.co.uk

Customers from outside the UK please telephone +44 1865 312262

Raintree is an imprint of Capstone Global Library Limited, a company incorporated in England and Wales having its registered office at 7 Pilgrim Street, London, EC4V 6LB – Registered company number: 6695582

Text © Capstone Global Library Limited 2011
First published in hardback in 2011
The moral rights of the proprietor have been asserted.

For The Brown Reference Group
Editorial Director: Lindsey Lowe
Managing Editor: Tim Harris
Editor: Jolyon Goddard
Original consultant: Dr. Mark Hostetler, Department of Wildlife Ecology and Conservation, University of Florida
Designers: Reg Cox, Joan Curtis
Picture Researcher: Clare Newman
Production Director: Alastair Gourlay
Printed in the USA

ISBN: 978 1 406 21837 4

14 13 12 11 10
10 9 8 7 6 5 4 3 2 1

**British Library Cataloguing in Publication Data**
Day, Trevor.
  Oceans and beaches. -- 2nd ed. -- (Biomes atlases)
  1. Marine ecology--Juvenile literature. 2. Coastal ecology--Juvenile literature. 3. Ocean--Juvenile literature. 4. Beaches--Juvenile literature.
  I. Title II. Series
  577.7-dc22

A full catalogue record for this book is available from the British Library.

The acknowledgments on p. 64 form part of this copyright page. Every effort has been made to contact copyright holders of material reproduced in this book. Any omissions will be rectified in subsequent printings if notice is given to the publisher.

**Disclaimer**
All the Internet addresses (URLs) given in this book were valid at the time of going to press. However, due to the dynamic nature of the Internet, some addresses may have changed, or sites may have changed or ceased to exist since publication. While the author and publisher regret any inconvenience this may cause readers, no responsibility for any such changes can be accepted by either the author or the publisher.

# About this Book

The introductory pages of this book describe the biomes of the world and then the ocean biome. The five main chapters look at different aspects of the ocean biome: climate, plants, animals, people and the future. Between the chapters are detailed maps that focus on major parts of the oceans. The map pages are shown in the contents in italics, *like this*. Exclamation-mark icons on the map pages draw attention to regions where the biome or its wildlife is under threat. Throughout the book you'll also find boxed stories or fact files about the oceans. The icons here show what the boxes are about. Words in **bold** throughout the book are explained in the glossary at the end of the book. After the glossary is a list of books and websites for further research and an index, allowing you to find subjects anywhere in the book.

 Climate

 People

 Plants

 Future

 Animals

 Facts

 Extinction

 Under Threat

# Contents

# BIOMES OF THE WORLD

Biologists divide the living world into major zones named biomes. Each biome has its own distinctive climate, plants and animals.

Desert is the driest biome. There are hot deserts and cold ones.

Taiga is made up of conifer trees that can survive freezing winters.

If you were to walk all the way from the north of Canada to the Amazon **rainforest**, you'd notice the wilderness changing dramatically along the way.

Northern Canada is a freezing and barren place without trees, where only tiny brownish-green plants can survive in the icy ground. But trudge south for long enough and you enter a magical world of conifer forests, where moose, caribou and wolves live. After several weeks, the conifers disappear, and you reach the grass-covered prairies of the central United States. The further south you go, the drier the land gets and the hotter the sun feels, until you find yourself hiking through a cactus-filled desert. But once you reach southern Mexico, the cacti start to disappear, and strange **tropical** trees begin to take their place. Here, the muggy air is filled with the calls of exotic birds and the drone of tropical insects. Finally, in Colombia you cross the Andes mountain range – whose chilly peaks remind you a little of your starting point – and descend into the dense, swampy jungles of the Amazon rainforest.

Scientists have a special name for the different regions – such as desert, tropical rainforest and prairie – that you'd pass through on such a journey. They call them **biomes**. Everywhere on Earth can be classified as being in one biome or another, and the same biome often appears in lots of

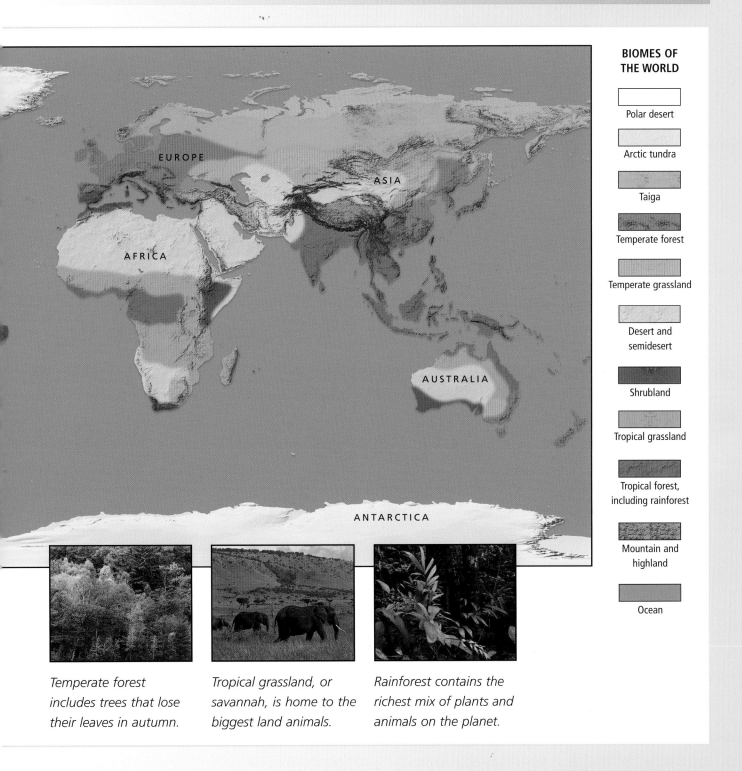

**BIOMES OF THE WORLD**

EUROPE
ASIA
AFRICA
AUSTRALIA
ANTARCTICA

Polar desert

Arctic tundra

Taiga

Temperate forest

Temperate grassland

Desert and
semidesert

Shrubland

Tropical grassland

Tropical forest,
including rainforest

Mountain and
highland

Ocean

*Temperate forest includes trees that lose their leaves in autumn.*

*Tropical grassland, or savannah, is home to the biggest land animals.*

*Rainforest contains the richest mix of plants and animals on the planet.*

different places. For instance, there are areas of rainforest as far apart as Brazil, Africa and Southeast Asia. Although the plants and animals that inhabit these forests are different, they live in similar ways. Likewise, the prairies of North America are part of the grassland biome, which also occurs in China, Australia and Argentina. Wherever there are grasslands, there are grazing animals that feed on the grass, as well as large carnivores that hunt and kill the grazers.

The map on this page shows how the world's major biomes fit together to make up the biosphere – the zone of life on Earth.

# OCEANS OF THE WORLD

Oceans cover more than two-thirds of Earth's surface, making the ocean biome the biggest biome of all. Under the waves, though, there are a multitude of habitats, from the beach to the deep-ocean floor.

The oceans are one gigantic body of water, but we give different names to different parts. The four major oceans are the Pacific Ocean, Atlantic Ocean, Indian Ocean and Arctic Ocean. Each lies in a huge hollow in Earth's crust, called a **basin**.

The oceans are not really one habitat, but a collection of habitats, many of which overlap. Most ocean plants and animals live near the coast, where the water is rich in **nutrients** from rivers, and where the shallow seafloor gets plenty of sunlight. Coastal habitats include forests of giant seaweeds, meadows of sea grass and some coral reefs.

Where sea meets land, another habitat exists: the intertidal zone. It can be a violent place, where savage waves continually crash into rocky cliffs. In other places, there are calm, sandy beaches that slope gently into the water. The animals and plants of the intertidal zone lead double lives, having to cope with being exposed to air and then being covered with water, at least once a day.

*The Pacific Ocean is dotted with coral islands in the tropics.*

*The Gulf of Mexico is fringed in parts with sandy beaches.*

Most of the open ocean has far less wildlife than the coast. Even so, the sea surface in places teems with microscopic creatures called **plankton**, which flourish in the sunlit water. Deep below the plankton is a zone of dark, cold water less rich in life but with some very unusual inhabitants.

## MAJOR SEAS AND OCEANS

1. Ross Sea
2. Pacific Ocean (see pages 28–29)
3. Arctic Ocean (see pages 54–55)
4. Gulf of California
5. Gulf of Mexico (see pages 18–19)
6. Caribbean Sea
7. Hudson Bay, Canada
8. Atlantic Ocean (see pages 8–9)
9. Weddell Sea
10. North Sea
11. Mediterranean Sea
12. Baltic Sea
13. Black Sea
14. Red Sea
15. Persian Gulf
16. Arabian Sea
17. Indian Ocean (see pages 44–45)
18. Bay of Bengal
19. East China Sea
20. South China Sea
21. Philippine Sea
22. Sea of Okhotsk
23. Japan Sea
24. Coral Sea
25. Tasman Sea

*Since the global ban on whaling, many species of whales are now thriving.*

*Monsoon winds carry sailboats along trade routes across the Indian Ocean.*

*Global warming is reducing the amount of ice covering the Arctic Ocean.*

The ocean floor is home to all sorts of animals. Many feed on dead matter raining from the waters above. Most seem to live near land, or on the summits of underwater mountains. Most of the seafloor has not been explored, so there could be many creatures far from land that we don't know about.

Recently, there has been much concern about the rise in temperature of the oceans. This is a result of **global warming** – the gradual warming of Earth's atmosphere because of the increase in pollutants in the air. If it continues at the present rate, global warming will result in the extinction of many marine animals.

# ATLANTIC OCEAN

Named after the Greek titan Atlas, who held up the heavens, the Atlantic is the second largest ocean. It stretches from the Arctic to Antarctica and contains about one-quarter of the world's seawater.

## Atlantic Facts

▲ The Atlantic Ocean is vast – it is about four times the size of North America.

▲ The average depth of the Atlantic is more than 3.3 kilometres (2 miles), or about 20 times the height of the Washington Monument in Washington, D.C.

▲ The Atlantic is deepest at the Puerto Rico Trench. It is 8.4 kilometres (5.2 miles) deep there, or 22 times the height of New York's Empire State Building.

▲ The Atlantic is getting wider at the rate of about 2.5 centimetres (1 inch) a year – about the same rate that your fingernails grow. The gradual movement of the Earth's continents is a natural phenomenon and is known scientifically as plate tectonics.

## Mid-Atlantic Ridge

During an expedition in the late 19th century, British scientists travelled widely across the oceans to sample their depths. The scientists discovered that parts of the Atlantic were much shallower than expected. At the time, some British newspapers declared that the scientists had found the fabled submerged city of Atlantis. In fact, they had stumbled across what was to be called the Mid-Atlantic Ridge. The east and west parts of the ocean floor are moving apart. The ridge forms where molten volcanic rock wells up from beneath Earth's crust and flows into the resulting gap. As the volcanic rock piles up, it forms a ridge. In places, the ridge is so high that it reaches the ocean surface, forming islands such as the Azores and Iceland. Today, we know that the Mid-Atlantic Ridge is just part of the huge mid-ocean ridge system that extends around the globe.

In addition to molten rock, superheated water gushes up from the mid-ocean ridge. The water is rich in minerals, which billow in dark clouds called black smokers (right). These smokers provide energy for strange forms of deep-ocean life.

Svalbard

GREENLAND

N

## Map labels

NORTH AMERICA
EUROPE
ASIA
AFRICA
SOUTH AMERICA
AUSTRALIA
ANTARCTICA

Hudson Bay

CANADA

ICELAND

Denmark Strait

Surtsey **1**

Cod fishing grounds **2** **(!)**

NORTH AMERICA

Grand Banks

**3** Bay of Fundy

Wreck of the *Titanic*

New England Seamounts

**4** Blake Ridge

**5** Gulf Stream

EUROPE

**7** BERMUDA

**6**

Madeira

Horseshoe Seamounts

Azores

Canary Islands

UNITED STATES

Gulf of Mexico

BAHAMAS

**8**

Sargasso Sea

CUBA

Caribbean Sea

Puerto Rico Trench

Hispaniola

Tropic Seamount

## Atlantic

AFRICA

CAPE VERDE ISLANDS

Mid-ocean ridge

Mouths of the Amazon River

SOUTH AMERICA

## Ocean

Ascension

**9**

Mid-ocean ridge

Columbia Seamount

Rio de Janeiro

São Paulo

Untreated sewage **10** **(!)**

Pacific Ocean

0 — 1,500 miles
0 — 1,500 kilometres

**12** Tristan da Cunha

Walvis Ridge

Benguela Current **11**

ANTARCTICA

## Numbered descriptions

### 7. Bermuda
Northerly coral reefs flourish here, warmed by the Gulf Stream.

### 8. Sargasso Sea
An area of ocean that remains relatively still on the surface, and where floating seaweed grows. The seaweed shelters and feeds animals, including camouflaged sargassum fish.

### 9. Mid-ocean Ridge
The Atlantic is spreading outward from the mid-ocean ridge, where new seafloor is forming. Hydrothermal vent habitats develop here.

### 10. Untreated Sewage
Hot spots for sewage pollution lie close to the large Brazilian cities of Rio de Janeiro and São Paulo.

### 11. Benguela Current
Cold, nutrient-rich water wells up here from the deep ocean. Plankton multiply and feed huge shoals of fish. Millions of sharks, tuna and seabirds thrive on the small fish.

### 12. Tristan da Cunha
The most remote inhabited land on Earth. The people here live 2,400 kilometres (1,500 miles) from the nearest human settlement (in South Africa).

### 1. Surtsey
In 1963, the volcanic island of Surtsey rose above the sea from close to the mid-ocean ridge near Iceland.

### 2. Cod Fishing Grounds
In the early 1990s, the great cod fisheries of the north-west Atlantic closed because there were too few fish left to catch.

### 3. Bay of Fundy
The tidal range here is 16 metres (52 feet) – the highest tidal range in the world.

### 4. Blake Ridge
A huge deposit of methane lies under the seabed here. Seeps of this gas support lifeforms that obtain energy from methane. There are mussel beds the size of a football field and mussels as big as footballs.

### 5. The Gulf Stream
A fast, warm current that flows from the Gulf of Mexico and crosses the North Atlantic. It helps make north-west Europe 10°C (18°F) warmer than places at the same latitude in Canada.

### 6. The Azores
These remote volcanic islands are surrounded by seas rich with life. Twenty-five types of whales and dolphins come here to dine.

**2**

*Cod is now rare in the northern Atlantic because of overfishing.*

# OCEANS AND CLIMATE

Oceans have a huge influence on Earth's weather. They also have their own underwater climates, which depend on a variety of factors, including ocean currents. Global warming has far-reaching effects on the oceans, too.

Seawater absorbs sunlight. Even in the clearest water, only about 1 per cent of the light reaches a depth of 100 metres (330 feet), and only the very surface of the ocean receives as much light as land. Sunlight is a mixture of different colours, which together appear white. The sea absorbs the different colours in differing amounts, screening some out but letting others pass. A scuba diver in a tropical ocean soon notices that the spectacular coral reef colours get less vivid the deeper he or she goes. Red and yellow get filtered out, making everything look blue-green.

## Beyond the Twilight Zone

Scientists divide the ocean into layers, or zones, based on depth. The top zone is the sunlit zone. As you sink through it, the light fades, the water gets cooler, and the pressure increases. At a depth of 200 metres (660 feet), there is barely any light left, and the pressure is 20 times higher than at the surface. This is the bottom of the sunlit zone.

*Conditions on the coast are dominated by the tides and the force of the waves. Over time, waves can carve bare rock into towering sculptures called sea stacks, like these at Cannon Beach in Oregon.*

Beneath the sunlit zone, down to 1,000 metres (3,300 feet), lies the twilight zone. The creatures of the twilight zone are often red or black, making them almost invisible in the gloom. But there are flashes of light because many animals, including twilight-zone fish and squid, produce their own light by a process called **bioluminescence**. They use this light to dazzle **predators**, to attract prey or to signal to other members of their **species**.

Beyond 1,000 metres (3,300 feet) deep is the dark zone – a world of total blackness, except for occasional flashes of bioluminescent light. This zone extends to the deep plains that make up most of the ocean floor. Pressures in the dark zone are more than 100 times greater than at the surface – enough to crush your lungs completely – and the water is bitterly cold, hovering between freezing point and 4°C (39°F).

## Ocean Facts

▲ Oceans cover 71 per cent of Earth's surface.

▲ The seas and oceans are slowly changing shape and size. The Pacific Ocean is shrinking, but the Red Sea is getting wider.

▲ Sea levels are rising, mainly because of global warming. This brings a risk of widespread flooding to coastal areas and many low-lying cities.

# Ocean Zones

Gannets

*Right: air-breathing divers usually stay less than 50 metres (160 feet) from the surface.*

### TIDAL ZONE

Peacock worm

Crab

Reef-building coral

### BEACH

Clam

### OPEN OCEAN
### SUNLIT ZONE

Move up at night

Move down during day

Sea turtle

Tuna

**200 metres**
**660 feet**

Zooplankton

Sperm whale

TWILIGHT ZONE

1

2

1. Jellyfish
2. Giant squid
3. Deep-sea anglerfish

**1,000 metres**
**3,300 feet**

3

DARK ZONE

Deep-sea brittle star

Deep-sea sponge

Deep-sea sea lily

## Tidal Zone
Whether it is rocky, sandy or muddy, the zone between high tide and low tide is home to creatures that attach themselves, burrow into the sediment or scuttle on top.

## Sunlit Zone
On the seabed below low tide lie coral reefs or sea-grass beds in the tropics or kelp forests in cooler seas. Tiny plantlike plankton drift in the surface waters, attracting grazers, which in turn attract predators such as tuna.

## Twilight Zone
Many open-ocean animals from tiny zooplankton to massive sharks hide in these dark depths during the day but visit the surface at night to feed.

## Dark Zone
These are hunting grounds for squid, anglerfish and other marine animals that scientists know little about.

## Seabed
There is life on the seabed at all depths. Even on the deep-ocean floor there is a thin rain of organic matter falling from the zones above that is filtered by sea lilies and sponges or scavenged by brittle stars.

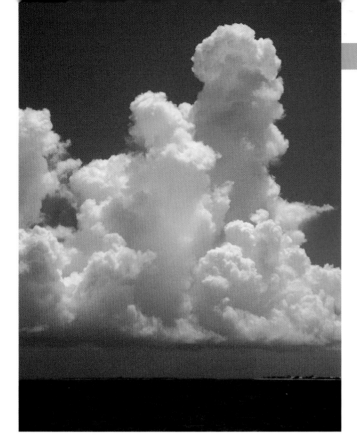

*Oceans play a central role in Earth's climate. Water escapes from the ocean surface as water vapour. It rises, cools, and turns to droplets, which form clouds.*

trenches, reaching depths of 10 kilometres (6 miles) or more. Life in the abyssal zone is similar to that in the dark zone, but pressures here are even more extreme. Only a handful of people in the deepest-diving submersibles have ever entered this world.

## Heat Sink

Compared to land, oceans warm up and cool down very slowly. As a result, they act as a gigantic heat store, able to absorb vast amounts of energy from the Sun in warm weather, and then release the heat slowly during cold weather. The oceans therefore have a huge influence on Earth's **climate**.

In warm, sunny parts of the world, the oceans pick up heat from the Sun. Ocean currents then carry this heat away and release it in cooler areas. Warm seawater flowing toward the North Pole, for example, keeps the Arctic Ocean warmer than it would otherwise be. Besides carrying heat around

Some of the animals here are miniature monsters: grotesque fish with swollen heads, gaping mouths and scrawny bodies. Food is so scarce that these fish try to eat everything they come across, dead or alive.

There is another zone below the dark zone: the abyssal zone. This is the deepest part of the ocean, where the seafloor plunges into deep

 ## Climate Change

The oceans have key roles in global warming and climate change. Rising sea levels are one of the more obvious effects of global warming. The oceans also play a vital role in the cycling of the element carbon. Vast stores of carbon lie beneath the oceans as oil and gas – the remnants of ancient lifeforms. The burning of oil and gas as fuels for humans releases this carbon into the air as the gas carbon dioxide. Increased levels of this gas in the atmosphere are the main cause of global warming. With more carbon dioxide in the air, more of it becomes dissolved into the oceans. This is changing the chemical balance of the seas, making them slightly more acidic. Some scientists believe that the increase in acidity is restricting the growth of coral reefs.

*Right: sea surface temperatures range from below 4°C (40°F), shown in black on this map, to above 27°C (80°F), shown in red. The warmest waters are near the equator, but where there are strong currents (white arrows), the ocean can be warmer or cooler than expected. The cold Humboldt (Peru) Current off the west coast of South America, for instance, causes a tongue of cool water to extend hundreds of miles toward the equator.*

## Rubbish Patch

Either side of Hawaii are immense areas of ocean containing human rubbish, mainly plastic, known as the Great Pacific Garbage Patch. Circular currents (gyres) in the Pacific concentrate the rubbish in swirling masses. Most plastic does not break down. Instead, it fragments into smaller pieces. These are a hazard to marine life. Millions of animals, including seabirds, die each year from eating the plastic, which they often mistake for food. Rubbish from the patch washes up on Pacific islands. Some beaches are covered up to 2 metres (6.5 feet) deep.

Investigations into tackling the problem have begun, but it may be impossible to clean up this area, which is the size of a small continent. Initial steps to clean the oceans could include banning the discharge of untreated sewage into the oceans, eliminating the use of plastic bags and finding alternatives to plastic. In 2007, San Francisco banned the use of disposable plastic bags in supermarkets. Other cities have since followed suit or started charging shoppers for plastic bags to discourage their use.

the planet, the oceans release water vapour into the air, producing the clouds and rain on which life on land depends.

## Rivers in the Sea

There are several reasons why ocean currents exist. One is simply that winds blowing on the ocean surface push the water along.

Winds exist because Earth's air is in constant motion, driven by the Sun's energy and stirred around by our planet's rotation. Air is continually circulating, travelling up and down in great circular patterns called circulation cells. The bottoms of these cells, where air moves along the planet's surface, form global winds. These, in turn, produce global currents in the ocean surface. One such current is the Gulf Stream, which flows across the Atlantic from the Gulf of Mexico to western Europe. The Gulf Stream transports nearly 500 million bathtubs full of water every second – several times the water passing through all the world's rivers put together. All that water carries a lot of heat, which keeps the climate of north-west Europe much milder than it would be otherwise.

## Merry-Go-Round

The major ocean currents flow in huge circles called gyres (shown on the map opposite), which are set spinning by Earth's rotation. Earth's rotation also makes the gyres turn in specific directions. In the northern hemisphere, the gyres turn clockwise. In the southern hemisphere, they

## El Niño

In most years, strong winds blow from east to west across the middle of the Pacific Ocean, driving the ocean current west. As warm surface water moves west, cool water wells up from deep below to take its place, bringing nutrients to the surface off the coast of Peru. The upwelling supports such vast shoals of anchovies that it forms one of the world's most important fishing sites. But in some years (left), the winds are weak. The upwelling does not develop, the anchovies don't come and the fishing is disastrous. The cool, nutrient-rich water is replaced by warm water from the western Pacific (white and red in the image). This is called an El Niño event. The El Niño event alters wind patterns around the world, causing extreme weather. It can also make the sea warmer, killing the organisms that build coral reefs. In recent years, 1988–1989 and 2006–2007 have seen strong El Niño episodes. Some scientists think that global warming is increasing the frequency of the El Niño event.

NORTH AMERICA

cool water

warm water   PERU

Pacific Ocean

turn counter-clockwise. One consequence of this is that in the southern Atlantic and Pacific, cold water from the poles extends along west coasts, while warm water from the equator usually travels along east coasts.

## Upwelling and Downwelling

Life in the oceans is richest where there is plenty of light, warmth and nutrients. The microscopic algae that live in surface waters – **phytoplankton** – need these to grow. But many parts of the open sea are like deserts.

Where there are few nutrients, there are few phytoplankton. And without phytoplankton, there are few of the animals that eat them.

There are oases in this desert. In certain places, a current of cold water from deep below, a process called **upwelling**, brings nutrients to the surface. Plankton grow in abundance at these places, providing food for fish and other animals. People also benefit from regions of upwelling – many of the world's fish are caught in these places.

Upwelling tends to happen on the eastern side of the great oceans. They are caused by offshore winds, which blow the surface waters out to sea. Deep waters full of nutrients well up from below to replace the surface waters.

What goes up must come down. Where ocean surface currents from opposite directions collide, some of the water is forced downwards in a process called **downwelling**. This water is usually clear because it has few nutrients and little plankton. The clear waters let plenty of light through, which is ideal for coral reefs. Some of the world's largest coral reef systems – those of the Caribbean and the Great Barrier Reef of Australia, for example – grow in regions of downwelling on the western side of oceans.

## Oceanic Conveyor Belt

Downwelling and upwelling areas are linked by deep currents flowing sluggishly through the oceans many thousands of feet down. These currents form what scientists call the oceanic conveyor belt – a continuous current of water that carries heat energy around the planet. The conveyor belt carries huge volumes of water and probably has a great effect on Earth's climate.

One downwelling region that feeds the oceanic conveyor belt is where the Atlantic Ocean meets the Arctic. Surface currents carry warm water from the Atlantic to the Arctic, where the water cools, freezes and floats. Salt is left behind when seawater freezes, so the

## Between the Tides

A rocky shore can be packed with all kinds of life, from seaweeds to crabs and sea anemones (right). A beach seems like a good place to live. But compared to the many thousands of different organisms that live in shallow water close to the shore, fewer species thrive on the beach. Why? Because life on a beach is tough.

A rocky beach is a frontier between land and sea. When the tide is out, the beach is exposed to the air – which can be far hotter or colder than the seawater. Marine organisms can dry out. If it is raining, animals are drenched in freshwater rather than salt water. And when beach animals are exposed to air, they can be attacked by land predators.

Life is still tough when the tide returns. Animals are battered by waves, and marine predators can then attack them. A barnacle or mussel fixed to a rock

cannot run away when conditions change – it has to stay there and put up with the changes. Sea anemones are also stranded. They choose hollows that become rock pools at low tide, or attach themselves in crevices that stay moist, withdrawing their tentacles to protect them from drying out. For those who can ride it out, the sea brings a fresh supply of food with each rising tide and for seaweeds there is plenty of sunlight.

*Warm surface currents (red) and cold, deep-sea currents (blue) are connected in a continuous stream of moving water called the oceanic conveyor belt.*

remaining water is cold and salty, which makes it heavy. This cold water sinks and begins its long voyage southward along the oceanic conveyor belt.

Global warming could disrupt this process. If ice stops forming in the far North Atlantic, the oceanic conveyor belt would be interrupted, with consequent climatic effects occurring across the globe.

## Hot or Cold

Temperature is one of the major factors that affects where sea creatures live. Birds and mammals are warm-blooded – they keep their bodies at a constant warm temperature, whether the surroundings are warm or cool. Warm-blooded animals such as whales can travel between warm and cold areas and still survive. Most sea animals are cold-blooded, which means their body temperature is affected by surroundings. Such species are less flexible about where they can live. Tropical fish would die in cold water, for instance, and cold-water fish cannot survive in tropical water.

*The Bay of Fundy, Nova Scotia, Canada, has the largest tidal range in the world. During the maximum high tide, the water is 16 metres (52 feet) higher than at low tide.*

# GULF OF MEXICO

From the sandy beaches and coral reefs of the coast to the mysterious chemical-energy communities of the deep-ocean floor, the Gulf of Mexico provides varied habitats for many kinds of marine life.

 ## Fact File

▲ Almost all adult female Kemp's ridley turtles – the rarest sea turtle in the world – nest each year at Rancho Nuevo beach in Mexico. These turtles are now protected and their numbers are increasing.

▲ Divers discovered the phenomenon of mass coral spawning in the Gulf of Mexico. Once a year, all the coral polyps release their eggs and sperm at once, creating an upside-down snowstorm. Scientists now study mass coral spawning the world over.

### 1. Rancho Nuevo
A beach where 95 per cent of Earth's population of Kemp's ridley turtles come to nest.

### 2. Flower Garden Banks
This U.S. National Marine Sanctuary protects an area of coral reefs. In 1990, divers here observed the snowstorm effect of a mass coral spawning for the first time.

### 3. Methane Seep
Scientists found ice worms, in 1997, living in a methane seep, where methane leaks into the ocean from under the seabed.

### 4. Meso-American Barrier Reef System
The second largest barrier reef on Earth lies off the coast of Belize. Countless billions of coral polyps built the reef by laying down their stony skeletons as they grew.

### 5. Yucatán Channel
Water flows into the Gulf of Mexico here, carrying plankton from the coral reefs of Belize.

### 6. Florida Keys
A long chain of low islands with coral reefs on the south side and sea-grass beds on the north. In 2009, scientists estimated that between 50–80 per cent of the living coral in the Florida Keys' reefs have been bleached or have died in the last ten years because of changes in the temperature of the sea.

### 7. Florida Bay
The sea-grass beds here are among the largest on Earth. Some of them are threatened by pollution. The beds are grazed by slow-moving manatees.

### 8. Florida Strait
Water flows out of the Gulf of Mexico through the Florida Strait, forming a current that eventually flows to Europe.

### 9. Bahamas
Scientists take part in the Wild Dolphin Research Program in the warm, shallow waters around the Bahamas island chain. They observe the social behaviour of the dolphins.

*Palm-fringed beaches with beautifully clear water are common in the Florida Keys. The main keys are connected by the Overseas Highway, one of the longest overwater roads in the world.*

UNITED STATES

Appalachian Mountains

Washington, D.C.

NORTH AMERICA
EUROPE
ASIA
AFRICA
SOUTH AMERICA
AUSTRALIA
ANTARCTICA

0          300 miles
0      300    kilometres

Atlantic Ocean

Houston

New Orleans
*Mississippi Delta*

MEXICO

FLORIDA

**2** *Flower Garden Banks*   **3** *Methane Seep*

**( ! )**

Monterrey   Rancho Nuevo

*Florida Bay*  **7**

Miami

Nassau

**1** **( ! )**   Gulf of Mexico

*Florida Keys*

**( ! )**  **6** → *Florida Strait*

**9**

B A H A M A S

Mexico City

Havana   **8**

C U B A

Guadalajara

*Yucatán Peninsula*

Yucatán Channel

CAYMAN ISLANDS
Cayman Trench

HAITI

JAMAICA
Kingston

**5**

Belmopan

B E L I Z E

**4** *Meso-American Barrier Reef System*

Caribbean Sea

GUATEMALA

HONDURAS

Guatemala City   San Salvador   Tegucigalpa

EL SALVADOR

NICARAGUA

Pacific Ocean

Managua

COSTA RICA

Barranquilla

PANAMA

San José   Panama City

COLOMBIA

## Lair of the Ice Worm

On the deep-sea floor in the Gulf of Mexico live some of the strangest animals known to science – ice worms (left). These pinkish worms, only 2–5 centimetres (1–2 inches) long, live in methane seeps, places where methane leaks into the ocean from deposits under the seabed. On land, methane is a gas, but in the cold and the high pressure of the seabed, it behaves strangely; it combines with water to form a kind of methane ice. It is in this unique habitat that ice worms live. They burrow in the methane ice and sculpt it into peaks like whipped cream. Scientists suspect that the worms live on bacteria. Some bacteria can use methane as a source of chemical energy to make food, just as plants use the energy in sunlight.

# PLANTS AND ALGAE

Most plant-like lifeforms in the oceans are not true plants at all. They are algae – such as seaweeds – which lack proper stems, leaves or roots. But like plants on land, they trap sunlight and use it to make food.

Plants on land are obvious – just take a look at the trees and grasses around you. But where are the plants in the oceans?

On some beaches you can find plant-like seaweeds – usually visible as brown, leathery ribbons washed back and forth by the waves. In some shallow waters, you can spot meadows of **sea grass**. But out at sea, you can't see any plants at all. They are there, but they are microscopic. They are single-celled marine **algae**. In a cup of seawater there are tens of millions of them.

Over the course of a year, the growth of these microscopic marine algae is greater than that of all the grasses and trees on land. Marine algae are really important – it's just that most of them are too small to see without using a microscope.

## Plankton

Most marine algae are plankton – organisms that drift along with ocean

*Coccolithophores are microscopic algae with intricate chalky shells that are made of overlapping plates. After they die, the shells fall to the seafloor, where they build up and gradually turn into chalk or limestone. These coloured microscope images show coccolithophores at 2,000 times their actual size.*

currents. Plankton, including algae, that can trap sunlight and use it to make food are called phytoplankton (*phyto* means 'plant').

When phytoplankton make food they also release **oxygen**, as do land plants. The whole process, called **photosynthesis**, is vital to most lifeforms, because they rely on the food and oxygen that plants produce. **Zooplankton** (animal-like plankton) eat phytoplankton, and larger animals such as fish and squid eat the zooplankton. Most of marine animals' food comes from phytoplankton. The smallest phytoplankton are incredibly tiny – hundreds would fit on a pinhead. Many are not algae but **bacteria**. Because of their size, these bacterial plankton slipped through scientists' nets, so nobody realised how common and important they were until recently. Phytoplankton produce more than three-quarters of the food and oxygen in any particular part of the sea.

Phytoplankton are under threat from global warming. In warm seas, fewer nutrients rise up to the floating phytoplankton, so these tiny lifeforms struggle to survive there.

SCOTLAND

## Plankton Blooms

Every spring, there is an explosion in the number of phytoplankton in the surface of the North Atlantic, brought on by warm, sunny weather. At its height, this 'plankton bloom' is so intense that the plankton are clearly visible from space. The bright blue-green patch of plankton in the picture lies off the coasts of England and France. The bloom fades in summer, and the dead plankton sink, forming a sludge that settles on the ocean floor.

All manner of worms, crabs and sea cucumbers feed on the fresh sludge. It also attracts swimming scavengers, from fish to small, shrimp-like creatures called amphipods.

IRELAND

ENGLAND

Plankton bloom

FRANCE

*Diatoms are minute algae that are found in all oceans. Their many complex shapes are formed by glassy skeletons.*

Phytoplankton are hugely important to all life because they absorb a lot of **carbon dioxide**, a gas that is necessary for photosynthesis. Their reduction in numbers in warm seas has a knock-on effect because an increase in the levels of carbon dioxide in the atmosphere – mainly from the burning of fossil fuels – is the major cause of global warming, which includes the warming of the oceans.

## Small but Beautiful

The medium and large phytoplankton are tiny, too. The largest are about the size of the full stop at the end of this sentence. Some, called coccolithophores, look like a tiny ball covered in round, chalky plates. When these plankton die and fall to the seafloor, their remains build up over millions of years to form a chalky carpet that can be hundreds of metres thick. England's famous White Cliffs of Dover formed this way from billions of coccolithophores. Phytoplankton come in many shapes. Diatoms, for instance, have skeletons made of silica, the main chemical in glass. Others, called dinoflagellates, have thinner skeletons shaped like leaves or cones. Many are bioluminescent – they produce their own light when the water is disturbed. In some parts of the world, the sea surface sparkles at night with the green light of dinoflagellates when waves break or when a person swims.

## Red Tides

Sometimes phytoplankton grow so quickly, and in such huge numbers, that they colour the water. As they die and become trapped on the surface, they form a scum. This is called a red tide. Despite the name, it can be any colour from yellow to blue.

Red tides can remove so much oxygen from the water that sea animals suffocate. And some red tides are poisonous. Shellfish, such as clams and oysters, can feed on the poisonous phytoplankton unharmed, but fish or other animals that eat the shellfish may die. Worldwide, red tides caused by a phytoplankton called *Alexandrium* kill nearly 200 people every year this way.

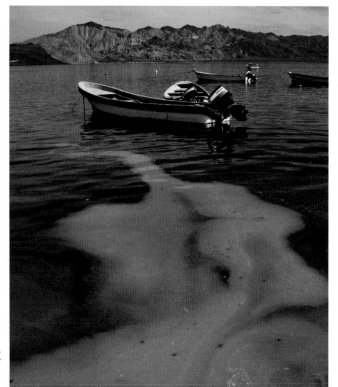

*Left: this is not a river of pollution but a red tide – a mass of tiny dinoflagellates. The cause of a red tide is usually natural, but sometimes the dinoflagellates multiply when land fertilisers run into the sea.*

*Kelp forests are full of dark corners for sea life to hide, so they are good places for divers to visit. This diver is filming in a California kelp forest.*

## Seaweeds

You can often find seaweeds attached to rocks in cool, shallow water. There are three different types – red, green and brown – depending on the coloured chemical used to trap light in photosynthesis. The biggest seaweeds are of the brown type and are called giant kelp. They are like underwater trees, towering up from the seafloor to the surface with fronds as long as 100 metres (330 feet). The smallest seaweeds, such as the bright green sea lettuce, are paper-thin. Other seaweeds form a tufted or crusty covering on rocks.

Large seaweeds have a tough time. Growing in shallow water, they have to resist the battering of waves and strong currents. They have to stay anchored to stop being swept out to sea. At the same time, they have to reach towards the surface to trap sunlight.

*Below: there are many types of kelp, but they all live in cool seas. They grow nearer the equator only where cold currents bring water from cooler regions. This happens on the west coasts of South America and Africa.*

NORTH AMERICA

EUROPE

ASIA

Atlantic Ocean

Pacific Ocean

Pacific Ocean

AFRICA

Equator

SOUTH AMERICA

Cold current

Cold current

Indian Ocean

AUSTRALIA

Major kelp beds

ANTARCTICA

A large seaweed is mostly three parts: a stem, fronds or blades (like leaves) and a holdfast. The stem and fronds are flexible so they can bend with the currents and waves. If they were rigid, they would easily snap. The holdfast, which looks a bit like a tangle of roots, anchors the seaweed to rocks on the seafloor. The fronds and the stem often contain air sacs, or bladders, that make the seaweed's fronds float.

## Help for Kelp

Lots of animals live among seaweed or attached to it, although few animals eat live seaweed. Many more feed on the thin covering of green algae that grows on the seaweed's surface.

In the North Pacific, there is a strange relationship between kelp and sea otters. Where sea otters live among the kelp, the kelp usually thrives, unless the water is polluted. But where sea otters are absent (perhaps because of hunting or pollution-related disease), the kelp seems to go through a boom-and-bust cycle. Sometimes it is abundant, but at other times it almost

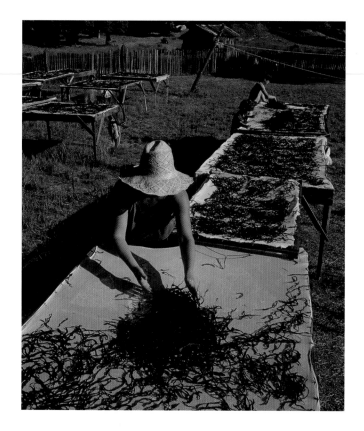

*Above: after being laid out to dry, this seaweed harvested in California might end up being used as a thickener in jelly and cosmetics.*

*Below: in parts of California, sea otter numbers are slowly recovering and healthy kelp forests are returning. The sea otter is called a keystone species – if it disappears from a habitat many other species are affected.*

disappears. Sea urchins – spine-covered animals related to starfish – seem to be responsible. Where sea otters are present, they feed on sea urchins and keep their numbers in check. Where otters are missing, sea urchins multiply and eat the kelp until there is almost none left. Without food, the sea urchins then die, and the kelp regrows.

## Kelp and Yogurt

What has kelp got to do with yogurt? Seaweeds – raw, cooked, or dried – can make delicious food. They are also rich in vitamins and materials. Not only this, seaweeds contain chemicals called alginates that are used in the food, medical, and cosmetics industries. Alginates form thickeners, binders, and stabilisers for all sorts of items: drug capsules, lipsticks, shampoos, toothpaste, low-fat mayonnaise and yogurts. Brewers also add them to pet foods and fruit pies.

## Sea Grass

Sea grasses are the only flowering plants that live underwater in the sea. They are true grasses, with proper stems, roots, leaves, and flowers. They grow best in clear, shallow water that has a soft bottom of nutrient-rich mud or sand. Where they grow well, they form large meadows that support many animals.

Few animals can eat the tough leaves of sea grass, but many use the leaves as a floating platform. If you examine a sea-grass leaf closely, you'll see green slime on the surface – a layer of microscopic algae. Snails, fish, and other animals graze on the algae. Many more creatures – tubeworms and sea squirts among them – attach themselves to sea-grass leaves and filter the passing water for the plankton on which they feed. These small animals, in turn, are eaten by crabs, fish, and other large animals.

In tropical waters, some sea urchins and parrot fish eat sea-grass leaves, as do some endangered animals, such as green turtles, manatees, and dugongs. Manatees and dugongs are also called sea cows. They are large mammals that look a bit like friendly walruses, though they are more closely related to elephants. They munch through energy-rich sea-grass roots as well as leaves.

*Knotted wrack, a type of kelp, holds itself afloat with tiny air bladders, which act like water wings.*

## Fact File

▲ The largest giant kelp can grow 30 centimetres (12 inches) a day.

▲ The total amount of kelp harvested every year in the United States for human use weighs 60,000 tonnes (65,000 tons), or as much as 10,000 African elephants.

▲ Overfishing damages kelp forests because fish eat the snails that eat the kelp. With fewer fish, the snails multiply and the forests suffer.

*Left: look closer at this delicate frond of seaweed and you'll discover it is in fact one of the world's most bizarre fish, called a weedy sea dragon. Its long, green fins camouflage it among kelp and sea grass.*

## Under Threat

Sea grasses are under serious attack – from humans. In some places, industries pollute seawater with oil or with heavy metals such as lead and zinc. All these pollutants kill sea grasses. Sewage also kills sea grass because it is very rich in nutrients – the nutrients make microscopic algae in the water multiply so much that they turn the water cloudy, depriving the sea grass of light. Fishing boats that dredge the seafloor for shellfish or drag fishing nets through sea-grass meadows also make the water cloudy.

A mysterious disease sometimes destroys sea grass. Scientists disagree on the exact cause of the disease, but some think it might be brought on by an increase in ocean temperatures caused by global warming. If sea-grass plants are already weakened by pollution, rising temperatures might be enough to finish them off.

In some parts of the United States, bays have lost more than half their sea-grass meadows in the last 40 years. Marine biologists are trying to reintroduce sea-grasses into areas where they were once abundant, but if global warming is causing the decline, the new plants are unlikely to survive.

Sea-grass meadows are not only important for wildlife. They also bind together mud and sand, and so help protect coastlines from being slowly worn away by the sea.

*The dugong is one of the few animals that can eat the tough leaves of sea grasses.*

*The bright blue flecks on the lips of this giant clam are algae. They produce food from sunlight, and pass some food to the clam. In return, the clam provides protection.*

## Strange Homes

Coral reefs – those dazzling, multi-coloured, fish-rich havens of tropical waters – would not be there but for microscopic algae. But where are the algae on the reef? They are inside the animals. Each coral **polyp** – the soft body of a living coral – contains microscopic algae called zooxanthellae – these can make up more than half the mass of coral polyps on a reef. The polyps give the algae a safe home in the sunlight, and in return, the algae give the polyps a supply of food, produced by photosynthesis. The algae also help the polyps produce their chalky armour. This close relationship, where both partners benefit, is a form of **symbiosis** (a close partnership between different species). The zooxanthellae are symbiotic algae. Without them, coral reefs would not exist.

The alga–polyp partners build their biggest reefs in clear, shallow waters in tropical seas, where the zooxanthellae can collect the most sunlight. Clear waters are found in downwelling regions where surface waters are poor in nutrients. Here, coral reefs grow particularly well.

Coral polyps are not the only sea creatures with plants inside them. Animals called sponges do the same thing. Giant clams – those that look as though they could grab your leg (but do not) – sport brightly-coloured bands of algae in their lips, where the two halves of the shell come together.

## Life Without Plants

Scientists once thought that all life depended on energy from the Sun. Plants and algae absorb the Sun's energy to make food, and animals eat them (or one another) to obtain the food. But another way of life is possible.

In 1977, scientists in a submersible on the floor of the Pacific Ocean, more than 1.6 kilometres (1 mile) below the surface, were looking for hydrothermal vents – places on the seafloor where volcanically heated water gushes into the ocean. They found something much more exciting. On the dark seafloor near a vent they came across huge, pale clams and dozens of giant worms – 1.2 metres (4 feet) long with red, feathery gills (right).

Scientists discovered that creatures living close to hydrothermal vents do not need sunlight or plants at all. They get all their food from bacteria that use energy from the chemicals in the vent water to make food. The giant worms and clams have bacteria inside their bodies. They give the bacteria a home and get food in return. The worms and clams grow much faster and larger than their relatives in shallow water.

# PACIFIC OCEAN

The Pacific is the world's largest stretch of water. It covers one-third of Earth's surface and contains about half the world's seawater. At its widest it is 17,700 kilometres (11,000 miles) across.

*Bora Bora lies near Tahiti in French Polynesia. Like thousands of other islands in the Pacific Ocean, it is an atoll made by coral fringing a collapsed volcanic crater.*

### 1. Japan's Fishing Grounds
People in Japan get half of their protein from fish. In 2009, the World Wildlife Fund for Nature warned that bluefin tuna would become extinct by 2012 because of overfishing.

### 2. Mariana Trench
This canyon's cold, dark floor is alive with shrimps, worms and micro-organisms.

### 3. Great Barrier Reef
This coral reef system may be the largest structure ever built by living organisms.

### 4. Emperor Seamounts
Seamounts are underwater mountains. Their tops provide isolated patches of submerged habitat that are cut off from other seamounts by deep ocean. Some harbour species that live nowhere else.

### 5. Midway Islands
These islands were the site of a battle in World War II (1939–1945), but are now a U.S. National Wildlife Refuge.

### 6. Kelp Forests
Seaweed forests formed by giant kelp. The kelp has recovered since a hunting ban allowed the sea otter to return. The otters eat the sea urchins that eat the kelp.

### 7. Juan de Fuca Ridge
Scientists found life teeming here in the 1980s, around hot vents in the ocean floor.

### 8. Monterey Bay
A National Marine Sanctuary stetching 640 kilometres (400 miles) along the California coast. People protect this area for the benefit of many species, such as sea lions and grey whales.

### 9. Gulf of California
This sheltered sea provides feeding grounds for finback whales. Grey whales also come here to give birth.

### 10. Galápagos Islands
These isolated islands have unique wildlife, such as seaweed-eating iguanas and flightless cormorants.

## Pacific Facts

▲ Mauna Kea is a volcano that rises from the Pacific Ocean floor to form the Big Island of Hawaii. Measured from its base it is 9.6 kilometres (6 miles) tall, which is taller than Mount Everest.

▲ Circular currents in the Pacific cause human trash, mainly plastic, to circulate in a swirling mass. Two vast areas, either side of the Hawaiian Islands, are known as the Great Pacific Garbage Patch.

▲ The deepest point on Earth is Challenger Deep in the Mariana Trench, which is 11 kilometres (6.9 miles) deep.

### 11. Galápagos Rift
In 1977, scientists first discovered hydrothermal vents here on the ocean floor. The vents spew out water hot enough to melt lead, but unique lifeforms cluster around them.

### 12. Humboldt Current
The Humboldt, or Peru, Current causes nutrients to well up from the deep and creates one of the richest fishing grounds on Earth. Penguins and seals hunt here, and sharks and tuna come to feast by the million.

Arctic Ocean

Laptev Sea

East Siberian Sea

Chukchi Sea

Beaufort Sea

N

RUSSIA

Sea of Okhotsk

Kamchatka Peninsula

Bering Strait

Bering Sea

Hudson Bay

NORTH AMERICA

Kelp Forests

Aleutian Islands (U.S.)

Aleutian Trench

(!) **6**

Sea of Japan

JAPAN

**1** (!)

Kurile Trench

Emperor Seamounts

**4**

**5**

**7**

Juan de Fuca Ridge

East China Sea

Izu Trench

Midway Islands (U.S.)

Hawaiian Islands (U.S.)

Monterey Bay National Marine Sanctuary

**8**

**9**

Atlantic Ocean

Philippine Basin

Challenger Deep

Mariana Trench

MARSHALL ISLANDS

Micronesia

Gulf of California

Gulf of Mexico

Caribbean Sea

PHILIPPINES

**2**

FEDERATED STATES OF MICRONESIA

Pacific

Galápagos Rift

**11**

PAPUA NEW GUINEA

NAURU

KIRIBATI

New Guinea

SOLOMON ISLANDS

TUVALU

Cook Islands (New Zealand)

Polynesia

(midocean ridge)

SOUTH AMERICA

**3**

Coral Sea

SAMOA

Galápagos Islands

**10**

Great Barrier Reef

AUSTRALIA

VANUATU

FIJI

TONGA

Tonga Trench

New Caledonia (France)

French Polynesia (France)

Bora Bora

Tahiti

Ocean

East Pacific Rise

Easter Island (Chile)

Peru – Chile Trench

Humboldt (Peru) Current

**12**

Pitcairn Islands (UK)

Southwest Pacific Basin

Tasman Sea

NEW ZEALAND

| 0 | | 2000 miles |
| 0 | 2000 | kilometres |

Pacific–Antarctic Ridge (midocean ridge)

ANTARCTICA

## Coral Bleaching

As ocean temperatures rise, so coral reefs become bleached and die. About 12 per cent of the corals in Fiji's Bequa Lagoon have died as a result of bleaching in recent years. After the water temperature at Papua Guinea's famous divespot, Kimbe Bay, reached 32°C (90°F), at least one in ten of the corals in the area became bleached. Reefs in Micronesia and Polynesia have also been affected. Some scientists believe Australia's Great Barrier Reef could disappear by 2030.

# OCEAN ANIMALS

Animals live at all depths in the oceans, from the surface to the seafloor 10 kilometres (6 miles) down. They range in size from the microscopic to the largest animal that has ever lived on Earth – the blue whale.

The oceans contain a vast amount of living space. They cover nearly three times as much of Earth's surface as does land, but they are more three-dimensional (3-D), with animals able to live at any depth. As a result, there is 6,000 times more living space in the oceans than on land.

## A Drifting Life

Animals that live floating near the ocean surface, among the plankton, are called zooplankton. Many are microscopic, but the largest, such as the biggest jellyfish, can be more than 1 metre (3 feet) wide, with tentacles 9 metres (30 feet) long.

Small and medium-sized zooplankton eat plant plankton (phytoplankton), which they catch in a variety of ways. Animals called **salps** and **larvaceans** pump seawater through their bodies, catching the phytoplankton in gel-like nets. Tiny, shrimp-like animals called **copepods** use hairy legs to waft phytoplankton towards their mouth.

Most large zooplankton eat smaller zooplankton. Arrow worms, for instance, are vicious killers, about 10 centimetres (4 inches) long. They dart after almost any prey smaller than themselves. Jellyfish capture fish and large zooplankton with their stinging tentacles. Not all large zooplankton are predators, though. Among the exceptions are krill – shrimp-like animals about 2.5 centimetres (1 inch) long that feed on phytoplankton. Krill are very common in antarctic waters, where they are the main source of food for many fish, birds and whales.

## Water Babies

Many ocean animals live in the plankton only when young, as **larvae**, and settle on the seafloor or seashore to grow into adults. Most larvae look completely different from the adults they will become. Barnacle larvae look

 ## How to Float

The trick in living among the plankton is to avoid sinking. Plankton use various techniques to stay afloat. One is to have lots of body projections, such as spines or hairs, to give the body a larger surface area. Another technique is to use droplets of oil or bubbles of gas to buoy up the body. Gel-like animals, such as salps and comb jellies, get rid of heavy chemicals and replace them with lighter ones.

With water to support their bodies, ocean animals have less need for a skeleton than do land animals. Octopuses have no bones whatsoever, allowing them to form their flexible bodies into endless different shapes and squeeze through tiny crevices. They use their suckered tentacles to grasp and smother prey.

# Insects of the Sea

The most common animals on Earth are not ants, flies or any other kind of insect, but tiny shrimp-like sea creatures called copepods, which also live in freshwater and wet places on land. Copepods outnumber all other animals on the planet. In their countless trillions, they probably outweigh any other type of animal, too. In the

oceans, they are one of the main sources of food for fish, making them of great ecological importance.

Copepods are members of a group of animals called crustaceans, which also includes shrimps, crabs and lobsters. There are almost no insects in the oceans, but crustaceans take their place.

*A puffer fish, or puffer (below), wards off attackers by inflating itself like a balloon (inset) and making sharp spines stand out on its skin.*

like fleas, some crab larvae look like miniature UFOs, and certain sea urchin larvae look like snowflakes. For animals that spend their adult lives on the seafloor or shore, having planktonic larvae is a good way of spreading to new areas because the larvae can drift great distances on sea currents.

Near the coast, at certain times of the year, planktonic larvae outnumber the normal residents of the zooplankton. Fish and other larger creatures gather together to take advantage of this bumper harvest.

## Fishy Business

The true kings of the ocean are fish. More than half of all living species of vertebrates (animals with backbones) are fish, and more than two-thirds of fish species live in the sea – at least 15,000 species. Fish are amazingly successful. They come in all shapes and sizes, from gobies less than 1 centimetre (0.5 inches) long to whale sharks reaching 18 metres (60 feet) – as big as whales. Fish live at all depths to about 6,000 metres (20,000 feet) down. Some can even breathe air and live on land or glide short distances over the waves.

Scientists classify fish into three main groups: those without proper jaws (lampreys and hagfishes); those with jaws and skeletons of cartilage (sharks and rays); and those with bony skeletons. The majority of fish belong to the bony group, including herring, cod, salmon, tuna and flatfish such as sole.

Though a few fish graze algae, most fish are predators – agile swimmers with sharp senses and strong jaws for snapping up food. Fish prey on everything from plankton to large sea animals, and many are skilled hunters. Some stun their prey with electricity, others hide and ambush victims, and many use speed and

agility to snatch prey from the water. Some of the sea's top predators are mammal- and fish-eating sharks – the most lethal fish on Earth.

## Shark Attack

Sharks have a bad reputation, but not all of them deserve it. Of the 400 or so species of sharks, about 40 species are known to have attacked people. In 2006, there were 62 unprovoked shark attacks recorded worldwide; four of the people involved died. In comparison, fishers caught millions of sharks in the same year and killed nearly all of them. Sometimes, fishers hunt sharks on purpose, but usually the sharks are unwanted, caught among tuna or other commercial fish.

Sharks use a range of senses to track down their food. They can smell blood from more than 1.6 kilometres (1 mile) away but use sight to identify victims nearby. Like most fish, they can feel the vibrations that travel through water, giving them a sense of touch at a distance. And from close range, they can detect the field of electricity generated by their victim's muscles.

Three species of sharks are responsible for most recorded attacks: the great white shark, the tiger shark and the bull shark. There are several reasons why these sharks might attack people. In some cases it is a case of mistaken identity – great whites occasionally attack surfboards, probably because they mistake the outline of surfer and board for that of a seal. In other cases a shark might attack if it feels threatened. Only rarely do sharks deliberately attack people in order to eat them.

In fact, you are much more likely to be run over by an automobile on the way to a beach than be killed by a shark when you get there. Nevertheless, swimming in waters where people have reported dangerous sharks is not a good idea.

## Coral Extravaganza

In the warm waters of the tropics are the most complex wildlife communities in the ocean: coral reefs. A single coral reef in the Pacific can contain more than 100 species of corals and several thousand species of

*Many corals live in large groups, sharing a skeleton and linked by sheets of tissue. The individual star-shaped animals, called polyps, emerge from the skeleton at night to catch plankton.*

*The great white shark's gaping jaws and jagged teeth enable it to kill seals, dolphins, and other prey with a single bite.*

*Arrowhead crabs live among the nooks and crannies of coral reefs. They use pincer-like claws to snip chunks of flesh off coral polyps and other animals.*

invertebrates (animals without a backbone), while providing a hunting ground for hundreds of fish species and other animals. The source of this abundance is the humble coral polyp, a tiny, tentacled animal that looks a bit like a flower. Coral polyps use their mobile tentacles to strain seawater for plankton, but they also obtain food from the algae that live inside their bodies (*see* page 27). Some polyps live on their own, but most clone themselves to form huge colonies in which all the individuals are joined together. Each coral species builds a colony of a particular shape – they might look like brains, mushrooms, antlers or giant plates. Corals sport all the colours of the rainbow – and the reef's other colourful inhabitants add to this palette, making a living reef an explosion of fascinating shapes and colours.

Many corals secrete a carbonate skeleton to protect themselves and support the colony. When the corals die, the skeletons remain in

*Bright colours are often a sign of danger. The frilly skin of many sea slugs contains microscopic stings, stolen from the sea anemones on which the slugs prey.*

## Coral Facts

▲ A barrier reef is a structure built by coral that lies parallel to the shore, on the far side of a lagoon.

▲ The largest coral reef system is the Great Barrier Reef of Australia. It is 2,000 kilometres (1,250 miles) long and clearly visible from space. It is made up of more than 2,500 separate reefs.

▲ The biggest coral atoll is Kwajalein in the Marshall Islands of the Pacific. It is more than 70 kilometres (44 miles) long and 32 kilometres (20 miles) wide.

▲ All coral reefs are under serious threat of survival from global warming.

place and gradually build up to form the reef. A coral reef's nooks and crannies provide havens where seaweeds and animals can settle and hide. Most reef animals graze the thin covering of algae that grows on the reef, or, like the coral polyps, they strain the water for plankton. Only a few animals, such as parrot fish and some starfish, can eat corals.

Some reef animals have their food delivered on a living plate. On many reefs there are cleaning stations where fish line up to have their skin, mouth and **gills** cleaned by fish and prawns that they might otherwise eat. The visitors seem to benefit by having parasites removed and wounds cleaned.

## World Without Light

More than 1,000 metres (3,300 feet) down, the sea is totally dark, except for light made by the animals themselves, or the headlights of submersibles carrying marine biologists.

For animals living in the dark zone, senses other than sight come to the fore. Most scavenging deep-sea fish find food by smell.

*Coral reefs (red) flourish in sunny, clear shallow water throughout the tropics, where the sea is warm. They grow near the coast and on underwater mountaintops.*

## Chemical Weapons

Many coral reef animals live fixed to one spot. They can't run away when danger threatens, so they need other ways of defending themselves when another animal wants to take a bite out of them. A popular strategy is to make chemicals that taste repulsive or are poisonous to predators.

Some of these chemicals have proved to be useful as drugs for treating cancer and other diseases. One example is ecteinascidin-743, which is now being used to treat several different types of cancers. It comes from a type of sea squirt, an invertebrate, living on coral reefs in the Caribbean. Another possible drug is discodermolide, which is being tested to halt the spread of tumors in the body. Discodermolide comes from a type of sponge, which is also found in the Caribbean.

*The huge, hinged mouth and elongated body of a deep-sea gulper eel make it look like a creature out of a nightmare.*

and viper fish can partially dislocate their jaws to swallow large meals. Many of these fish have a stomach that stretches, allowing them to swallow prey bigger than themselves.

Those hunting live prey can also feel the telltale ripples and vibrations in the water that other animals make. The long, sensitive tendrils of some deep-sea anglerfish and the elongated fins on tripod fish's heads are suited to this purpose. Some fish can even detect the tiny electrical signals produced by their victims' muscles.

Anglerfish have another trick up their sleeve. Instead of hunting down their prey, they use a glowing lure, attached to a long stalk on the head, to draw victims towards them. The lure looks like a wiggling worm – an irresistible temptation to hungry animals. When a victim comes into striking range, the anglerfish snatches it in its massive jaws.

Many deep-sea creatures depend for food on the snowfall of dead animals, body parts and feces from high above. Even so, food is very scarce, and animals must conserve their energy. Deep-sea fish move very little, and their muscles are small and puny compared to those of other fish. But they make up for this by the size of their mouth and stomach. Gulper eels, or deep-sea swallowers, have vast jaws and a snake-like body,

*Animals of the deep have to catch whatever they find. Viper fish (far right) have monstrous, cage-like teeth to trap hatchet fish (above right) and other prey.*

## Finding a Mate

Besides being pitch-black, the deep-sea world is enormous and mostly empty. Because food is hard to find, animals are scattered much further apart than in surface waters. The darkness and emptiness can also make it difficult for fish to find mates. Many probably use their sense of smell to zero in on scent chemicals (pheromones) produced by a potential mate. At close range, anglerfish can identify suitable mates by the pattern of light from the glowing lure, and other fish species probably recognise light patterns, too.

Once an animal has found a mate, it is all too easy to lose it again in the inky blackness. Some male anglerfish have a drastic solution to this problem: they sink their teeth into the female's body and stay attached for the rest of their lives. In such species, the male is much smaller than the female. The female's skin grows over the male, and he becomes a parasite, feeding on her blood.

## Making Light Work

Many animals in the twilight zone, and some in the dark zone, can produce their own light (bioluminescence). This comb jelly, for instance, produces shimmering, rainbow-coloured lights along its transparent body. Bioluminescent light comes from a chemical reaction in special light organs and is usually blue or green. It has a variety of uses. Some deep-sea squids squirt out a cloud of shimmering light that distracts an attacker, giving the squid a few seconds to escape. Anglerfish use a luminous lure to catch prey, and lantern fish sport complex patterns of lights that help them recognise other members of their species. Some fish of the twilight zone have lights on their underside. Seen from below, the spots of light help camouflage them against the faint glow of the sea surface.

## Mysteries of the Deep

Even today, there are probably many undiscovered animals in the oceans. With the ocean so difficult to study, and with so much water to search, it is not surprising that animals, even large ones, remain to be seen.

Marine scientists only encountered the weird animal communities of deep-sea vents in 1977. In 1997, they discovered something even weirder: worms living inside frozen methane gas on the floor of the Gulf of Mexico. And one species of whale – the True's beaked whale – was only found alive at sea in July 2001. A male leaped 24 times out of the water near a ferry in the Bay of Biscay, France. Luckily, there were whale experts on board to witness and photograph the event.

For centuries, most scientists thought the giant squid was a myth. But in the 1850s, a Danish zoologist decided to examine the reports of sightings and analyse samples. He soon confirmed that the creature was real – it was a giant version of the common squid.

In 2006, Japanese researchers filmed a giant squid swimming in its natural habitat. There is a type of squid even larger than the giant squid. It is called the colossal squid. As yet, it hasn't been filmed in the wild, but several specimens have been washed up on beaches or caught by fishers. The colossal squid has a bulkier body than the giant squid,

## A Living Fossil

In 1938, fishers caught a strange, stocky fish, about 1.5 metres (5 feet) long, off eastern South Africa. The skipper took the fish to the local museum curator, Marjorie Courtenay-Latimer, who recognised it immediately. Nobody believed her when she said it might be a coelacanth – a fish believed to have been extinct for 60 million years. Luckily, she had the foresight to have the fish stuffed, and when fish expert J. L. B. Smith came to examine it, he could hardly believe his eyes. The coelacanth's internal organs had been thrown away when it was stuffed, so Professor Smith began searching for an intact specimen – a hunt that took another 14 years. In 1998, coelacanth enthusiasts discovered a second species – this time off Indonesia. Who knows what other large sea creatures remain undiscovered?

# Ocean Discoveries

The oceans are so vast, deep and unexplored that all sorts of mysterious creatures might lurk in their depths, awaiting discovery. The finding of animals such as giant squid, megamouth sharks and unknown whales continues to amaze experts. Some of these creatures were previously known, but only from long-dead fossils.

### 1. Megamouth Shark
In 1976, this large-mouthed shark was found entangled in a parachute in the sea near Hawaii. It feeds on plankton near the sea surface at night, but descends to the depths during the day, which explains why it is so rarely seen.

### 2. Six-Eyed Spookfish
This fish looks like a pike but has six eyes. It was discovered in 1958, at a depth of more than 100 metres (330 feet).

### 3. Monoplacophoran
Scientists dredged this shelled mollusk, which looks like a giant limpet, off Mexico's west coast in 1952. Biologists thought its kind had died out 350 million years ago.

### 4. Vestimentiferan Worm
In 1977, scientists discovered hundreds of huge tube worms, up to 2 metres (7 feet) long, among dozens of other new species of fish, clams shrimps, and crabs at deep-sea vents.

### 5. Ice Worm
In 1997, scientists discovered this new species of worm living in methane ice on the floor of the Gulf of Mexico.

### 6. Lesser Beaked Whale
Parts of this whale's body were first found near a fish market in San Andres, Peru, in 1976. Several complete specimens were later found, and it was officially described as a new species in 1991.

### 7. Vampire Squid
This tentacled, purple-black animal was caught in an Atlantic deep-sea sample in 1903. In 1946, scientists confirmed it is neither a true squid nor an octopus, but a member of a related group thought to have been extinct.

### 8. Giant Squid
The giant squid that lives in the North Atlantic grows to 13 metres (43 feet) long. Its larger relative, the colossal squid, lives in the oceans around Antarctica.

### 9. True's Beaked Whale
The first confirmed sighting of a living True's beaked whale took place in July 2001 in the Bay of Biscay, off France.

### 10. Deepwater Stingray
The first specimen washed up on a South African beach in 1980.

### 11. Coelacanth
The first live specimen known to science was caught near South Africa in 1938. At that time, the only other coelacanth specimens were fossils as old as dinosaurs.

and adult females (which are larger than males) are thought to grow to 14 metres (46 feet) long. With these discoveries, scientists are continually having to rewrite their textbooks.

## Marine Migrations

Many marine animals make incredibly long journeys to find food or to breed. These epic voyages are called **migrations**.

Most migrations are seasonal. At a certain time of year, the animal migrates to a new home, where conditions are better for the next stage in its life cycle. It might migrate to breed, for instance, but then return later in the year to somewhere better for feeding.

Salmon and freshwater eels not only migrate through the sea but also travel up rivers. This is a challenge, because freshwater contains far smaller concentrations of chemicals than salt water. The move requires changes in the animal's body function.

Several species of Pacific salmon lay their eggs in the gravel-covered beds of North American rivers. When the baby fish hatch, they set off downriver, and grow into adults by the time they reach the ocean. Years later,

## Living in Sand

At the very edge of the ocean is the shore, where conditions for animals such as this clam change drastically: the seabed is exposed twice a day by the tide. Unlike rocky shores, where hardy sea life survives attached to rocks, sandy shores often appear devoid of life. But they can be full of animals – beneath the surface. Most sandy-beach animals burrow, especially at low tide, to avoid predators and to avoid drying out. Many clams stay buried at high tide, too, but extend their siphons (tubes) into the water. The siphons pump the water and filter out food particles.

siphons

the adults return to breed in the exact place where they hatched. To get there, they must swim upstream through rapids and leap up waterfalls. They must avoid all sorts of natural and artificial obstacles – dams, fishing nets, anglers, bears and pollution.

When they arrive at the breeding grounds, they scoop out a gravel nest. The female lays her eggs, a male fertilises them, and then both male and female die.

Atlantic eels make a reverse journey. Adults lay their eggs on the floor of the Sargasso Sea – a still patch of the Atlantic Ocean near Bermuda. The young eels rise to the surface, drift on ocean currents and swim into North American and European rivers. They mature in lakes and rivers, and then return to the Sargasso Sea to breed.

*The endangered hawksbill turtle roams the tropical oceans. When it is time to mate and lay eggs, it travels to one of only a handful of nesting sites worldwide.*

Both salmon and eels are under threat from global warming. Warmer rivers and oceans result in a higher percentage of the fish dying before reaching their reproductive age.

Many seabirds, sea mammals and turtles make journeys just as long as those of eels and salmon – or even longer. The Arctic tern flies an astonishing 32,000 kilometres (20,000 miles) each year on its round trip between the Arctic Ocean and Antarctica. It breeds on the Arctic coast in summer, but flies south in autumn to spend the rest of the year in the ocean around Antarctica, where it is summer at this time.

*Spinner dolphins can swim at 40km/h (25 mph). They hunt in packs, rounding up small fish such as herring into tight shoals before moving in for the kill.*

Grey whales breed in the Gulf of California in winter, away from the attentions of killer whales (orcas), which hunt in cooler waters. In summer, adults and calves swim north to the Arctic, where food is more abundant. In total, the whales swim up to 20,000 kilometres (12,500 miles) each year – the longest migration of any mammal.

Green turtles born on Ascension Island return as adults to this tiny island in the

 Gone Forever

The last recorded sighting a Caribbean monk seal was in 1952. After an extensive search by marine biologists, the seal was finally declared extinct in 2008. These large seals – up to 2.7 metres (9 feet) long – lived in the tropical waters of the Caribbean and off the Bahamas and Yucatán Peninsula. Their docile nature and curiosity on land made them an easy target for human hunters, who were responsible for their demise.

Atlantic Ocean. They travel 2,200 kilometres (1,370 miles) from feeding grounds close to Brazil to mate in the waters off Ascension. The females then come ashore to lay eggs.

## Marine Mammals

Fish may be the kings of the oceans, but the biggest sea creatures are whales. Whales belong to a class of animals called mammals, which also includes dogs, bats, elephants and humans. Mammals are warm-blooded animals that breathe air and feed their young on milk. They evolved on land about 210 million years ago, but about 65 million years ago, some began living in the sea.

The first marine mammals were fierce meat eaters that looked a bit like crocodiles. Over millions of years, these crocodile-like mammals became streamlined, their stumpy legs became fins and their hair gradually disappeared. Although they still have to come to the surface to breathe, they have now mastered the oceans. They are the cetaceans: whales, dolphins and porpoises.

Some cetaceans – the toothed whales– hunt fish, squid and other sea mammals. These cetaceans are fast and agile swimmers, and have teeth for gripping their prey. Dolphins, killer whales, porpoises and sperm whales are all toothed whales. Some toothed whales have large brains and may be highly intelligent.

Bottle-nosed dolphins may even solve problems by thought, and they sometimes use tools. In the shallow seas off the coast of western Australia, bottle-nosed dolphins hold a sponge in their mouth to protect their snout while they dig for shellfish.

Other cetaceans – the baleen whales – have a giant sieve (a baleen plate) inside the mouth instead of teeth. These whales take massive gulps of seawater and squeeze it through the sieve to collect small animals, such as krill. Baleen whales are the giants of the ocean. The blue whale, which weighs up to 190 tonnes (209 tons) and reaches up to 33 metres (110 feet) long, is probably the largest animal that has ever lived on Earth.

Some baleen whales sing to one another to communicate. Humpback whales are famous for their long, haunting songs and their co-operative hunting techniques. In the breeding season, adult males sing a 20-minute song to attract females and to intimidate other males. In polar waters, groups of humpbacks blow curtains of bubbles to herd schools of fish and krill into a tight ball. Then they lunge upwards through the close-packed school – a bumper harvest for little effort.

*Humpback whales, although among the largest of animals, eat only tiny prey – krill and small fish. In one mouthful, they swallow many thousands.*

# INDIAN OCEAN

The Indian Ocean formed about 125 million years ago when Africa tore free from Antarctica and drifted north. Now this ocean's wonders include coral islands, Antarctic breeding grounds and giant river deltas.

*In late 2004, an earthquake off the coast of Sumatra triggered a tsunami that resulted in the deaths of about 300,000 people in coastal regions of the Indian Ocean.*

## Monsoons

In the northern Indian Ocean, the winds nearly always blow from the ocean to the land in summer, bringing very wet weather to the land. In winter they reverse, blowing from the land and making the weather hot and dry. Winds blowing in this seasonal pattern are called monsoons, and they have a profound influence on the climate of the countries around the Indian Ocean. The wind direction is so constant that dhows, the ancient sailing vessels of the northern Indian Ocean, do not come equipped with adjustable sails. The sailors must lower and re-attach the sail when the wind changes direction or the boat needs to sail on a new course. In other parts of the world, sails are readily adjustable because sailors are used to changeable winds. The dhow to the right is sailing to the island of Zanzibar off east Africa.

## Fact File

▲ The Portuguese explorer Vasco da Gama sailed across the Indian Ocean in 1497, after rounding the southern tip of Africa. Ever since, the Indian Ocean has been a trade route for silks, rugs, tea and spices.

▲ The yellow-bellied sea snake swims throughout the Indian Ocean and into the Pacific. But like other tropical life in the Indian Ocean, it can't reach the Atlantic due to the cold sea around southern Africa.

Caspian Sea

ASIA

CHINA

**3** Persian Gulf

Mouth of the Indus River

Ganges River Delta

CHINA

Red Sea

Arabian Peninsula

INDIA

Bay of Bengal

South China Sea

Arabian Sea

Andaman Islands (India)

Nicobar Islands (India)

Gulf of Thailand

PHILIPPINES **7**

**9**

AFRICA

Aldabra

**!**

**1** **2**

SEYCHELLES

Zanzibar

COMOROS

**!** **5** MALDIVES

Indian

SRI LANKA

Ocean

**!** **11**

Sumatra

**!** **7**

MALAYSIA

Borneo

**7**

Sulawesi

INDONESIA

British Indian Ocean Territory (UK)

Java Sea

Java

**9**

MADAGASCAR

Réunion (France)

Rodrigues (Mauritius)

MAURITIUS

Ninetyeast Ridge

**6**

Java Trench

Cocos Islands (Australia)

Christmas Island (Australia)

**8**

Ningaloo Reef

AUSTRALIA

Shark Bay

**10**

Southwest Indian Ridge

**4**

Kerguelen (France)

0        1,000 miles
0     1,000     kilometres

## 1. Aldabra
A coral atoll that is a U.N. World Heritage Site. It is home to the Aldabra giant tortoise, robber crabs and land hermit crabs.

## 2. Seychelles
The Seychelles lost most of its living coral reefs after the El Niño event of 1998. The coral is slowly recovering, but like other tropical reefs the coral is threatened by global warming.

## 3. Persian Gulf
Vast oil reserves lie under the shores and seabed of this gulf.

## 4. Kerguelen
Many mammals and birds of the southern Indian Ocean breed here. Albatrosses, seals and penguins abound.

## 5. Maldives
Growing coral reefs keep these low-lying islands above water, but nowhere are they higher than 1.8 metres (6 feet). Rising sea levels threaten their future.

## 6. Java Trench
This canyon is 7.45 kilometres (4.6 miles) deep, the same as 19 Empire State Buildings.

## 7. Cyanide and Dynamite Fishing
Population growth in Southeast Asia has led to destructive fishing methods around the coral reefs of Indonesia. Fishers kill fish for the food market with dynamite, and use cyanide to stun fish for the pet trade.

## 8. Ningaloo Reef
Warmed by a tropical ocean current, this long coral reef fringes the coast of Australia. Visitors come to watch migrating whale sharks, the world's largest fish.

## 9. Indo-West Pacific
Thousands of species of animals, plants and micro-organisms from both the Indian and Pacific oceans mingle in this area.

## 10. Shark Bay
The world's largest sea-grass bed, more than 120 kilometres (75 miles) long and home to dolphins, sharks and dugongs.

## 11. Epicenter of Sumatra-Andaman Earthquake
The 2004 quake caused a tsunami that killed 300,000 people.

# OCEANS AND PEOPLE

Many thousand of years ago, our ancestors used the oceans only as a source of food. Later they became proficient sailors and crossed the seas to explore and colonise the whole world.

The first long-distance sailors may have been the people who colonised the islands of the western Pacific Ocean. Around 6,000–7,000 years ago, people sailed east from New Guinea to the Solomon Islands, and by 3,500 years ago they had reached the middle of the Pacific Ocean. To get there, they would have sailed huge distances beyond the sight of land.

While Pacific islanders were bravely setting out across the ocean, the seafarers of Africa and Europe were much more cautious, and generally sailed close to the coast. Even so, they made some daring voyages.

According to the Greek historian Herodotus (484–425 B.C.), explorers from Phoenicia (now Lebanon) sailed all the way around Africa in about 600 B.C. Helped by regular stops to obtain provisions, the sailors took

three years to make the epic voyage.

Among the greatest early seafarers of Europe were the Vikings – the people who lived in Scandinavia between the years 500 and 1100. In the 8th century C.E., Vikings attacked towns in Britain, Ireland and France, spreading fear throughout the countryside. But some Vikings came to farm and trade and not to pillage.

In about the year 1000, Vikings set off west from Greenland. Eventually they reached a forested coast that they called Markland, which means 'land of woods'. Today, historians believe this to be southern Labrador, Canada – which means that Vikings discovered the Americas nearly 500 years before Christopher Columbus did.

## Age of Exploration

Starting in the 15th century, a series of Portuguese sailors set off on major voyages to set up new trade routes and find new lands to colonize. Historians call this period the Age of Exploration. In 1486, Portuguese sailor Bartholomeu Dias became the first known European to sail around the tip of Africa from west to east. In 1498, Vasco da Gama sailed from Portugal to India, opening up sea trade between Europe and Asia.

One of the world's most influential sea journeys took place in 1492. Italian explorer Christopher Columbus led a Spanish-sponsored expedition to

*Left: the Phoenicians built a sea empire by controlling trade routes across the Mediterranean Sea. Their ships and sailors were the best in the Mediterranean.*

find the western route to the East Indies (Southeast Asia). After five weeks, his three ships landed on an island in the Bahamas – Columbus had crossed the Atlantic. On his heels came many other expeditions, with John Cabot from England reaching mainland North America in 1497.

It might seem that ocean travel is less important today than it used to be, but nothing could be further from the truth. More than 90 per cent of bulk goods – everything from fruit to refrigerators – travels in the hold of cargo ships rather than in aircraft. In your household, many of the foods and domestic items (or their parts) travelled by sea at some stage.

## Undersea World

Explorers have now mapped every square mile of Earth's land surface, but they have barely begun to explore the mysteries of the undersea world.

*One of the oldest ways of making use of the sea is spearfishing. It is still common in parts of the tropics, including this bay in Madagascar. Besides spearing fish, the fishers cast small nets or look for squid and crabs while wading through the water.*

## Around the World

After pioneering voyages of the 15th century by explorers such as Columbus, the time was ripe for someone to try to sail all the way around the globe. In 1519, Portuguese nobleman Ferdinand Magellan left Spain in five small ships (right). His aim was to sail west to the Spice Islands (the Moluccas in Indonesia) to claim them for Spain.

Magellan assumed that the islands were not far beyond the Americas – he had no idea that the world's biggest ocean, the Pacific, lay in the way. During the 100-day crossing of the Pacific, the crews were reduced to eating rats and mice, chewing leather and drinking

soup made with wood shavings. When the sailors arrived in the west Pacific, they met an unfriendly reception. Islanders stole their provisions, and Magellan himself was killed by islanders in the Philippines.

Two ships did reach the Spice Islands in November 1521. But only one made it back to Spain, arriving in September 1522. Of the 237 men that had set out on the expedition, just 18 completed the amazing around-the-world trip.

→ Bartholomeu Dias, 1486
→ Christopher Columbus, 1492
→ John Cabot, 1497
→ Vasco da Gama, 1498
→ Ferdinand Magellan, 1519–1521

ASIA

INDIA

Cochin

Philippines

Moluccas

AUSTRALIA

The earliest records of diving come from Mesopotamia (now Iraq). About 6,500 years ago, Mesopotamian divers were holding their breath for two minutes and plunging 10 metres (33 feet) to gather shellfish. In the 4th century B.C., the Greek philosopher and scientist Aristotle described a type of diving bell that used metal breathing pipes. It is not clear exactly how, or if, the device worked.

The first good description of a working diving device dates from around 1700. At this time, English scientist Edmond Halley designed a diving bell made of wood. It enabled divers to recover objects from shipwrecks. Helpers sent fresh air down in barrels, while divers explored underwater and returned to the bell at short intervals.

In the 19th century, diving suits became a better option than diving bells. In 1837, the German Augustus Siebe invented the metal helmet and diving suit that you see in old Hollywood adventure movies. Divers using this equipment could descend much farther 60 metres (200 feet) and with much greater mobility than those using diving bells.

## Scuba Diving

In 1943, two Frenchmen – explorer Jacques Cousteau and engineer Émile Gagnan – revolutionised diving with a new invention:

*Replicas of Columbus's ships sail past Florida's Kennedy Space Center in 1992 to mark the 500th anniversary of Columbus's first voyage across the Atlantic.*

scuba (self-contained underwater breathing apparatus). Thanks to scuba, divers are now free to explore underwater without being encumbered by breathing tubes connected to the surface. However, because the body can't safely absorb nitrogen or oxygen gas at very high pressure, scuba diving is limited to depths of about 60 metres (200 feet) with air, or 185 metres (610 feet) when breathing a mixture of oxygen and helium. To dive beyond this, some divers have tried filling their lungs with oxygen-rich liquid to prevent the pressure crushing the lungs. During their dive, they continue to breathe the liquid, their lungs acting like gills.

## Submarines and Submersibles

A Dutch inventor named Cornelis Drebbel is thought to have built the world's first working submarine. Drebbel's craft was a completely enclosed wooden boat, covered with greased leather to make it waterproof. Oars extended through tight-fitting leather flaps in the sides and provided the only means of propulsion. Between 1620 and 1624, Drebbel took his submarine on test runs in the Thames River in England, rowing it along about 4 metres (13 feet) below the surface. He is said to have taken King James I for a ride in it. People now use a variety of underwater

*Right: before the invention of scuba gear, divers had to wear very bulky suits and stay attached by hoses to air tanks on the surface.*

*Below: today, both snorkellers and divers use lightweight masks and wetsuits and plunge into the oceans for fun – but diving remains a dangerous sport.*

craft to explore the oceans. Scientists increasingly use *remotely operated vehicles* (ROVs), which don't contain a crew and can be piloted from a ship. ROVs remain attached to a mothership by cables, but the latest submersibles – called *autonomous underwater vehicles* (AUVs) – are completely free moving. These small, robotic craft can be programmed to stay underwater for long periods, carrying out research.

## Ocean Resources

The oceans are full of valuable resources. Many, such as the minerals on the bottom of the sea, are difficult and expensive to gather. But more accessible resources, such as fish, have been massively overexploited in most parts of the world and some fish stocks are in serious decline.

Water itself is a valuable commodity. In the United States, the average person consumes about 570 litres a day for drinking, cleaning and flushing the toilet – about 200 times the amount used by a person in Equatorial Guinea in Africa.

Seawater is too salty for drinking or watering crops. However, in places where there is little freshwater, desalinisation facilities can be used. These use sunlight to turn seawater to water vapour. When seawater **evaporates**, it leaves its salt behind. The desalinisation plant collects the freshwater vapour and turns it back to liquid.

Worldwide, humans get less than a tenth of their food from the oceans. But this fraction is important, because seafood is a major source of **protein** in tropical countries, where other protein sources are scarce. Oily fish, such as salmon and mackerel, are very healthy to eat. These fish are rich in certain fats that help lower people's blood **cholesterol** levels. Lower cholesterol means a reduced risk of heart disease and stroke.

## Fished to the Limit

Each year, catches of certain marine fish get smaller, although fishers keep trying harder to catch them. Fishers remove more fish from the oceans than are replaced by breeding.

As a result, many of the world's fish supplies are in decline.

## Into the Abyss

The deepest point in the oceans is the Mariana Trench – a vast canyon on the floor of the Pacific Ocean. In 1960, Frenchman Jacques Piccard and American naval lieutenant Don Walsh descended to the bottom of the Mariana Trench in a submersible called *Trieste*. Their craft consisted of a ball-shaped metal compartment slung below a submarine-shaped tank filled with gasoline, for buoyancy. After 5 hours, the craft touched bottom at 10.9 kilometres (6.8 miles). The uncrewed, remotely controlled *Nereid* explored the trench in 2009.

These days, submersibles such as *Deep Rover* (right) are kept busy by scientists eager to explore the unknown deep sea, and by engineers inspecting cables and pipelines on the seabed.

## Saving the Planet

One answer to the overfishing problem is fish farming. Salmon and trout farms have already lowered the price of these fish drastically, and the fish are no longer luxury items. Some fish farmers rear fish in net cages suspended in the sea, while others build seawater ponds close to the shore. Today, fish farming accounts for about a quarter of all marine produce. However, there are drawbacks.

Keeping fish crowded together encourages fish diseases to prosper, so farmers have to dose the fish with antibiotics. Parasites, such as fish lice, also thrive in the crowded conditions. Some scientists are concerned that fish lice from farmed salmon are devastating natural populations of salmon in the northeast Atlantic. The wastes from farmed fish also affect the environment. They contain nutrients that make phytoplankton grow rapidly, altering the balance of the natural biological community.

Governments know that overfishing is causing serious problems, but they cannot agree on how to manage fishing. The industry is a bit like a gold rush, with different countries catching as many fish as they can before the supplies run out. In the process, fish populations are decimated. When there are no more fish left to catch, the fishers lose their jobs or hunt elsewhere for new fish stocks to exploit. So the cycle continues. The United Nations recently estimated that most of the world's important fishing areas were either overfished or fished to the limit.

## Minerals from the Sea

The salt in seawater is another valuable commodity. Ever since people started farming and eating a lot of cereals and vegetables, they have used salt in their diet. People still gather salt by channelling seawater into shallow ponds where the sunshine turns the liquid to vapour, leaving the salt behind.

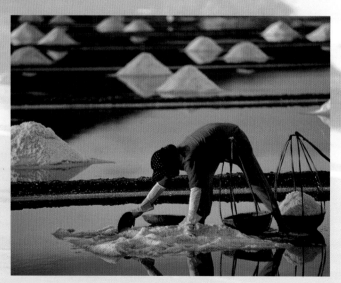

*Left: in Vietnam, people let seawater evaporate and collect by hand the salt that is left behind. This woman first piles up the salt, then collects it when it is dry.*

*Drilling rigs can reach oil deep beneath the seabed. Natural gas (methane) often comes up with the oil, so the gas is burned off to prevent an explosion.*

Even more important than solid minerals are the oil and gas supplies that come from reserves under the seafloor. Oil and gas drilled from below the sea provide more than 40 per cent of the world's supply of these fuels. As supplies from land get used up, oil and gas exploration moves into ever deeper waters.

Most of the other chemicals in seawater are in amounts too small to be worth harvesting, even though some of these substances are valuable. In some places, minerals such as gold and diamonds are eroded from rocky shores by the sea. They are sifted and sorted naturally by waves and currents to settle near the shore, where they are mined. Surprisingly, however, people make more money from sand and gravel than from any other solids mined from the sea. House and road builders use these materials for making concrete and for many other purposes.

*Today, tourism and leisure are among the most important ways of using the oceans. Surfing, diving, sailing and fishing have all become multi-million dollar industries.*

 Resource Facts

▲ Between the 1600s and 1980s, whaling reduced the populations of the largest whales, including blue whales, to a tenth of their former number.

▲ There is enough gold dissolved in the oceans to provide everyone in the world with a lump weighing about 4 kilograms (9 pounds).

# ARCTIC OCEAN

At the top of the world is the Arctic Ocean, surrounded by continents on all sides. Ice formed by the freezing of seawater covers almost the entire Arctic Ocean in winter, and only powerful ice-breaking ships can pass through.

## Arctic Crossing

As late as the 1890s, many geographers thought that a continent lay at the North Pole, or at the very least, that the Arctic was a shallow sea. Norwegian scientist and explorer Fridtjof Nansen was one of the few who did not. Nansen designed the *Fram*, a boat that would rise up out of the ice rather than be crushed by it. Between September 1893 and August 1896, the *Fram* drifted with the Arctic ice, at one point coming to within 400 kilometres (250 miles) of the North Pole. Nansen and a companion set out for the Pole on foot but had to turn back in severe weather and spend winter on the ice. Nansen's expedition proved that there was no major continent in the Arctic, just ocean. Recent satellite images have shown that it would be possible – as a result of global warming – to sail through broken ice and now reach the North Pole in late summer.

*Global warming has decreased the polar bear's habitat. Less sea ice means fewer seal pups – the main prey of polar bears – which live on the ice.*

## Fact File

▲ Even in summer, half the Arctic Ocean is covered in sea ice, much of it more than 3 metres (10 feet) thick. However, global warming is significantly shrinking the amount of ice in both summers and winters. Scientists fear that there will be ice-free summers in the Arctic by 2030.

▲ Every year at the North Pole, six months of darkness is followed by six months of light.

▲ When the great glaciers that flow off the Greenland ice cap meet the ocean, large chunks of ice, or icebergs, break off and float away. Once free, the icebergs drift south in the Atlantic.

## 1. Bering Strait
A narrow passage between Alaska and far eastern Siberia.

## 2. Chukchi Sea
Walrus mothers and their calves migrate through the Chukchi Sea. Oil exploration in the sea threatens many animals in this remote part of the world.

## 3. Polar Abyssal Plain
This deep plain lies 4.6 kilometres (2.9 miles) beneath the arctic ice. That's 50 times the height of New York's Statue of Liberty.

## 4. Route of the *Fram*
The route of Norwegian explorer Fridtjof Nansen's ice-bound voyage in 1893–1896.

## 5. Word Hunt Island
Intrepid travellers often begin their North Pole expeditions here.

## 6. Resolute Bay
'Near threatened' beluga and narwhal whales pass by on their way to their summer feeding grounds. The small village of Resolute stands on the shore.

## 7. Permanent Ice Sheet
The ice sheet in the middle of the ocean breaks up, at its edges, into fragments called pack ice. Global warming is causing shrinkage of the ice.

## 8. Svalbard
People live on this remote group of islands. Some of the inhabitants still hunt whales.

## 9. Greenland Coast
Chilly arctic water flows close to this coast and keeps it ice-bound for most of the year.

## 10. Norwegian Coast
Atlantic water, warmed by the Gulf Stream and North Atlantic Drift, keeps the Norwegian coast free of ice although it is well within the arctic circle.

## 11. Greenland Icebergs
The International Ice Patrol tracks Greenland icebergs that might endanger shipping. The biggest icebergs reach about 450 metres (1,500 feet) high and nearly 1.6 kilometres (1 mile) long, with two-thirds or more lying unseen underwater.

# THE FUTURE

Everyone has a role to play in the fate of the oceans. What food we eat, how we get rid of rubbish and where our fuels come from all have an impact on the health of our seas.

The 2000s were the warmest decade on record. Most scientists believe the global climate is getting warmer. If so, the likely cause is an enhanced greenhouse effect.

The greenhouse effect is a natural process that has been happening for billions of years. It is caused by gases in the **atmosphere** called greenhouse gases. When sunlight strikes Earth's surface, much of the energy is absorbed and then emitted back into space as heat. Some of the outgoing heat gets trapped in the atmosphere by the greenhouse gases, warming the planet.

*Low-lying coral islands, including entire nations such as Tuvalu, could drown if sea levels rose as a result of excessive global warming.*

The most important greenhouse gases are water vapour, carbon dioxide and methane.

In the last 150 years, pollution has raised the level of some greenhouse gases. Extra carbon dioxide released by the burning of fossil fuels (coal, oil and natural gas) has raised carbon dioxide levels in the atmosphere by more than a quarter. This has made the greenhouse effect stronger, possibly triggering global warming.

## Rising Seas

Earth's climate goes through cycles over thousands of years. Sometimes factors combine to make the global climate cooler. When this happens, snow falls instead of rain and stays on the land instead of running into the sea. Ice builds up at the poles, and water in the oceans shrinks slightly as it gets cooler. As a result, sea levels fall. Scientists describe such times as ice ages, or glacials.

At other times, the global climate warms. When this happens, seawater expands, polar ice melts and sea levels rise. We are in the middle of one of these warm periods, called an interglacial. Since the peak of the last ice age, some 18,000 years ago, global sea levels have risen by 120 metres (394 feet) – that's more than the height of the Statue of Liberty.

According to scientists' predictions, global warming could make Earth's climate some 2.5°C (4.5°F) warmer during the 21st century. The rise in temperature would make Earth's seawater expand slightly, and more polar ice could melt, so sea levels would rise. Many small tropical islands, such as the Marshall Islands in the South Pacific and the Maldives in the Indian Ocean, lie only 1–2 metres (3–6 feet) above sea level. Such islands could disappear underwater within the next few centuries. Large

areas of Bangladesh, bordering the Bay of Bengal, are less than 2 metres (6 feet) above sea level. Here, floods from storm waves already endanger many millions of people.

## Poisoning the Seas

Pollution from land often ends up in the sea. Some pollutants are dumped there, others run into the sea through rivers and air pollutants fall into the sea with rain.

Oil pollution is most obvious when a tanker runs aground and spills its cargo into the sea. But oil pollution is happening all the time at a low but harmful level: the amount of oil running into the sea from land is nearly ten times that from major tanker spills.

Some forms of pollution are particularly dangerous because they build up in the bodies of marine animals. This happens especially with dissolved heavy metals

## Climate Change

Many scientists are worried that global warming is causing polar ice to melt faster. Most of Earth's ice is on land, on Greenland and Antarctica. If it melted more quickly, more water would run into the sea and sea levels around the globe would rise. For example, if the Lesser Antarctica ice sheet were to collapse, sea levels would go up by about 5 metres (17 feet). Low-lying cities such as Miami would disappear under the sea. This scenario is unlikely in the near future, but there are many uncertainties about the pace of global warming. If the larger Greater Antarctica ice sheet ever collapsed, sea levels would rise by at least 52 metres (170 feet).

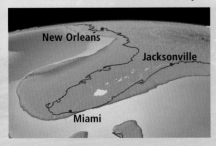

*Sea level 18,000 years ago, 120 metres (394 feet) lower than today's.*

*Possible future sea level, 5 metres (17 feet) higher than today's.*

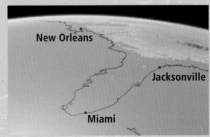

*Possible future sea level, 52 metres (170 feet) higher than today's.*

*Some ships discharge their waste into the sea routinely. The ocean near ports and harbours is often heavily polluted.*

and artificial chemicals that are organic (carbon-based) and contain chlorine. These organic chemicals include by-products from plastics manufacture, such as PCBs, and pesticides, such as DDT. PCBs might be responsible for the mysterious mass deaths that sometimes affect seals, sea lions and dolphins. In recent years, hundreds of dolphins have been washed up on the east coast of the United States. Scientists found unusually high levels of PCBs in their bodies.

Global warming and pollution are not the only threats facing the oceans. Another is habitat loss – the destruction of fragile marine habitats, such as sea-grass meadows, coral reefs and kelp forests. The worst habitat destruction occurs near shores or in shallow water, and the damage is often hidden from view. Trawling for fish and shellfish can strip the seafloor of almost all larger forms of life. It disrupts the lives of burrowing worms and shellfish, and it stirs up mud, smothering many small, bottom-living creatures.

## Coral Grief

Coral reefs are very sensitive to human activities. Pollution and muddy water running into the sea from towns can kill coral. Tourists and fishers can damage coral by simply touching it, by standing on it or by dragging anchors or cables across it. Many reefs are overfished. Sometimes traders stun exotic fish with cyanide to gather them for the aquarium trade; the cyanide kills the coral.

In recent years, coral reefs have suffered from a mysterious condition called bleaching. The

*This African penguin is a victim of an oil spill. It will probably fatally poison itself while trying to clean oil from its feathers.*

*Mass fish deaths can be a sign of a major pollution incident. Fish may be killed by toxic chemicals that leak into rivers and reach the ocean at estuaries.*

coral organisms lose the microscopic algae that live inside them, which makes the coral turn a stark white, as though bleached. Death often follows. Scientists are not sure what causes coral bleaching, but many suspect a rise in sea temperature, caused by global warming, is to blame.

## Lack of Action

At the 1992 Earth Summit in Rio de Janeiro, Brazil, many governments signed an agreement called the Convention on Climate Change, with the aim to cut the release of greenhouse gases. Progress since then has been slow, with factories in many countries still belching out greenhouse gases. Countries are still struggling to agree on cuts in carbon dioxide emissions to halt global warming – as witnessed at the 2009 United Nations Climate Change Conference, held in Copenhagen, Denmark.

 Saving the Planet

The future for the oceans is not all bad news. Since the 1960s, governments across the world have set up more than 1,300 protected marine areas, though many of these are small and are not particularly well protected from activities such as overfishing. Since 1994, most governments have also agreed to obey rules drawn up by the United Nations to protect the oceans. Meanwhile, scientific organisations such as the Intergovernmental Panel on Climate Change continue to monitor the oceans and publish findings, and many non-governmental organisations, such as the World Wildlife Fund, raise awareness about marine pollution, overfishing, overhunting and habitat loss.

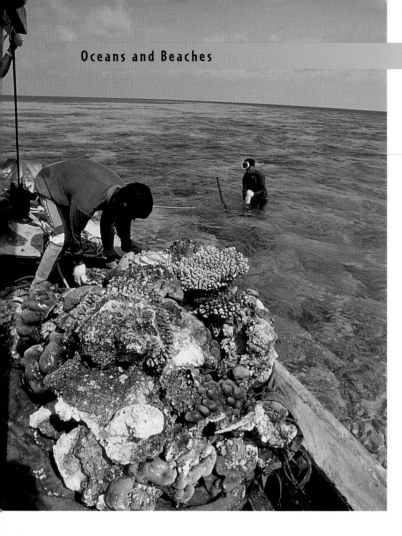

Above: in Malaysia, as in many other countries, people deliberately remove coral for souvenirs or blow it up with dynamite for use as building material.

## Fact File

▲ The World Wildlife Fund for Nature states that a quarter of the world's coral reefs are now damaged beyond repair and another two-thirds are under serious threat from human activities and global warming.

▲ Worldwide, fishers lose or discard more than 100,000 tons of netting and line each year. Many marine animals become entangled in the nets and die.

## Energy from the Sea

The oceans contain many resources that could prove useful in the future. One is energy. The heat stored in the oceans, and the constant movement of seawater, are vast sources of energy that have been barely tapped. The technology to harness tidal power already exists. The Rance Estuary Barrage in France, for example, generates electricity by capturing the power of the tide. Each tide produces enough electricity for tens of thousands of homes.

Only a handful of tidal power stations have been built so far. At this one in France, the tide flows through the barrage at the far end, where the fast tidal current churns the water into white peaks. As the water passes, it drives turbines, which generate electricity.

## Underwater Hotel

It might seem ridiculous to suggest that underwater hotels will one day exist, but some already do. At Jules Underwater Hotel in Florida, visitors enter the hotel through an opening some 9 metres (30 feet) below the sea surface, and can watch tropical fish swimming past their bedroom windows. The whole building is entirely underwater, propped up by legs on the bottom of a mangrove lagoon. In development are Poseidon Undersea Resorts, the first of which will open in Fiji, and the huge Hydropolis, which lies 20 metres (66 feet) under the Persian Gulf (in Dubai) and will have 220 suites.

Ocean energy sources cause less pollution than power stations driven by fossil fuels, but there are drawbacks. Wave-power stations are expensive to build, for instance, because they need to be strong enough to withstand storms but light enough to work with small waves. And tidal power stations can damage coastal habitats by altering the way the tide covers and uncovers beaches and mudflats.

## New Minerals

Scattered over large areas of the deep-ocean floor are potato-sized lumps of valuable metals, such as cobalt, manganese, copper and nickel. These lumps, or nodules, form over millions of years as dissolved metals slowly crystallise out of seawater. The nodules are worth trillions of dollars, but they are too expensive to harvest because they lie at least 4 kilometres (2.5 miles) underwater. One day, when the demand for these metals is great enough, and mining technology is more advanced, the nodules may be scooped from the seafloor.

There are also metal deposits at vents in the seabed, sometimes in shallower water. Old vents that have stopped spurting hot water (and that no longer provide homes for the remarkable vent-living animals) could one day be mined. They are rich in zinc, copper and even silver and gold.

The oceans are not just a pleasant place to visit – they are vital for the health of our planet. They provide an indispensable part of our food supply, but more than this, the circulating oceans, and the organisms within them, create our weather and our climate.

# GLOSSARY

**alga (plural algae)** a simple, plant-like organism that makes food from sunlight like a plant but lacks proper roots and leaves

**antibiotic** a substance, often a drug, that kills bacteria

**atmosphere** the layer of air around Earth

**atoll** a ring-shaped coral reef formed above a submerged volcanic island

**bacterium (plural bacteria)** a single-celled micro-organism; among the tiniest and simplest forms of life

**basin** a bowl-shaped depression on land or the seabed

**bioluminescence** light created by living organisms

**biome** a major division of the living world, distinguished by its climate and wildlife. Tundra, desert and temperate grasslands are examples of biomes

**carbon dioxide** a gas released when fuel burns. Carbon dioxide is one of the main gases causing global warming.

**cholesterol** a waxy chemical in the human body. When too much is present, it can block arteries.

**climate** the pattern of weather that happens in one place during an average year

**community** a collection of organisms living in the same place, such as a sandy beach or a reef

**copepod** a tiny shrimp-like animal that forms a major part of the animal plankton of the oceans

**delta** a wide, typically ¢-shaped plain at the mouth of a river where sediment collects

**downwelling** the downward movement of surface water to the depths of the ocean

**ecological** to do with the way organisms interact with one another and the environment

**equator** an imaginary line around Earth, midway between the North and South poles

**erode** to gradually wear away land by the action of wind, rain, rivers, ice or the sea

**estuary** a place where the tide mixes with freshwater from a river, usually in an inlet of the sea at the mouth of a river

**evaporate** to turn into gas. When water evaporates, it becomes water vapour, an invisible part of the air.

**gills** organs that enable animals to breathe underwater

**global warming** the gradual warming of Earth's climate, caused by pollution of the atmosphere

**ice age** a period when Earth's climate was cooler and the polar ice caps expanded. The last ice age ended 10,000 years ago.

**lagoon** an area of shallow water sheltered by a stretch of land

**larva (plural larvae)** a young form of an animal. A tadpole is the larva of a frog.

**larvacean** a tadpole-like marine animal related to sea squirts

**mangrove** a tree that grows in swamps on tropical coasts. Many mangroves have prop roots to support themselves.

**methane** a gas that occurs naturally under the seabed. Also called natural gas, people sometimes use it as a fuel.

**migration** a long-distance journey by an animal to find a new home. Many animals migrate each year.

**nutrient** any chemical that nourishes plants or animals, helping them grow. Marine plants absorb nutrients from seawater. Animals get nutrients from food.

**oxygen** a gas in the air. Animals and plants need to take in oxygen so that their cells can release energy from food.

**photosynthesis** the chemical process that plants and algae use to make food from simple chemicals and the sun's energy.

**phytoplankton** plant-like members of the plankton, such as microscopic algae

**plankton** organisms that drift along with ocean currents, mainly near the surface.

**polyp** a coral animal. Polyps are usually tiny but live together in large colonies of various shapes.

**predator** an animal that catches and eats other animals

**protein** one of the major food groups. It is used for building and repairing plant and animal bodies.

**rainforest** a lush forest that receives frequent heavy rainfall

**salp** a gel-like, jet-propelled sea animal related to sea squirts

**sea cucumber** a cigar-shaped relative of starfish. Many sea cucumbers resemble dill pickles.

**sea grass** a true flowering plant that grows in meadows on seabeds just below low tidemark

**seamounta** a submarine mountain rising from the seabed. Even its peak is underwater.

**seep** a place on the seabed where chemicals such as oil and methane slowly enter the ocean

**spawn** to release lots of small eggs. Many fish and coral spawn.

**species** a particular type of organism. Cheetahs are a species, but birds are not, because there are lots of different bird species.

**symbiosis** an intimate partnership between two living organisms. Both partners may benefit, or only one may benefit.

**temperate** having a moderate climate. Earth's temperate zone lies between the warm tropical regions and the cold, polar regions.

**tidal range** the difference in height between high and low tide

**trench** a canyon in the seabed

**tropical** within about 2,575 kilometres (1,600 miles) of the equator. Tropical places are warm all year.

**tropical forest** forest in Earth's tropical zone, such as tropical rainforest or monsoon forest

**tropical grassland** a tropical biome in which grass is the main form of plant life

**tundra** a biome of the far north, made up of treeless plains

**upwelling** a kind of vertical ocean current that brings water from the depths to the surface

**vent** a hole in the seabed where high-pressure hot water and minerals enter the ocean

**zooplankton** animal-like members of the plankton

# Further Research

## Books

Byatt, A., Fothergill, A., and Holmes, M. *The Blue Planet: Seas of Life*. New York: DK Publishing, 2001.
Earle, Sylvia A. and Lindstrom, Eric. *Atlas of the Ocean: The Deep Frontier*. Washington, D.C.: National Geographic Society, 2001.
Marx, Christy. *Life in the Ocean Depths (Life in Extreme Environments)*. New York: Rosen Classroom, 2009.
Rose, P., Laking, A., and Cousteau, P. *Oceans: Exploring the Hidden Depths of the Underwater World*. Berkeley: University of California Press, 2009.

## Websites

NOAA Ocean Explorer: oceanexplorer.noaa.gov
(Follow the National Oceanographic and Atmospheric Administration as they explore the deep ocean.)
Sea and Sky: www.seasky.org/sea.html
(Packed with pictures, sounds and information about the ocean, this is a colourful, fun multipurpose site.)
Nova Online – Into the Abyss: www.pbs.org/wgbh/nova/abyss
(Another fun exploration of the deep ocean.)
National Marine Sanctuaries: sanctuaries.noaa.gov
(Links to educational sites, photos and information about the marine world.)

# INDEX

## Picture Credits

Key: l – left, r – right, m – middle, t – top, b – bottom.

Front cover: Getty Images: Jeff Hunter/Imageba.
Ardea: Kurt Amsler 60t; Francois Gohier 7l; Art Explosion: 32 (inset), 35t, 35b, 42b; Bruce Coleman: Pacific Stock 14, 31, 32b, 34/35, 36, 53b, 58t; Rinie van Meurs 26b; Jim Watt 26t; Corbis: 49; Frank Lane Picture Agency 30; Stephen Frink 27t; Wolfgang Kaehler 47; Buddy Mays 6r, 18; Jeffrey L. Rotman 23, 34; Kevin Schafer 22b; Phil Schermeister 24t; Nik Wheeler 7m, 44b; Ralph White 27b; Digital Stock: World Panoramas 16/17; Eberley College of Science: Penn State 19; Fisheries Industres of the United States by George Brown Goode 42b; Hulton/Archive: Central Press 50m; Image Bank: John William Banagan 52b; istockphoto: 9, 13b; Jules' Underwater Lodge: 61t, 61 (inset); La Ranc 60b; Lamont-Doherty Earth Observatory: William Haxby 57b/l, 57b/m, 57b/r; Mary Evans: 46, 48; NASA: 11 (inset), 15; Jacques Descloitres, MODIS Land Rapid Response Team/GSFC 21; NHPA: Martin Harvey 58b; Trevor McDonald 25; Norbert Wu 38t; NOAA/OAR/NURP: 39; P. Rona 8; University of Hawaii/T. Kirby 51; PhotoDisc: Robert Glusic 4m; Bruce Heinemann 5l; Jeremy Hoare/Lifefile 56/57; Jack Hollingsworth 5m; Doug Menuez 53t, 58/59; Photolink 5r, 7r, 13t, 24b, 33, 42t, 43; Russell Illig 10/11, 16 (inset); Kim Steele 41; Karl Weatherly 4r; Shutterstock: Melvin Lee 29; Kang Khoon Seang 52t; A. S. Zain 44t; Still Pictures: Roland Birke 32t; Manfred Kage 22t; Jeffrey L. Rotman 50b; Secret Sea Visions 12; Norbert Wu 38b; Stone: Paul Chesley 6m, 28; Thinkstock: Photos.com 54.

The Brown Reference Group Ltd has made every attempt to contact the copyright holder. If anyone has any information please contact info@brownreference.com